CW00732276

THE MYSTICAL LANGUAGE
OF ICONS

Solrunn Nes

THE MYSTICAL LANGUAGE
OF ICONS

ST PAULS

ST PAULS Publishing
187 Battersea Bridge Road, London SW11 3AS, UK

Copyright © ST PAULS 2000

ISBN 085439 584 9

Icon painting and text: Solrunn Nes
Wood work: Mietek Dembowiak
Photography: Sture Nepstad
Design: Solrunn Nes in cooperation with
Jan Ole Tveit

Produced in the EC
Printed by Società San Paolo, Roma, Italy

ST PAULS is an activity of the priests and brothers
of the Society of St Paul who proclaim the Gospel
through the media of social communication

Front cover:
Christ Immanuel
Model: mosaic from San Marco, Venice
Egg tempera on wood. 26, 5 x 52 cm (1992)

Page 5:
Mandylion
Greek variant
Egg tempera on wood with papyrus surface
13 x 18 cm (1997)

Page 7:
Standing Christ Pantocrator
Greek variant
Egg tempera on oak. 21 x 47 cm (1996)

Page 16:
Christ the Saviour
Russian variant
Egg tempera on oak. 17, 5 x 24 cm (1995)

CONTENTS:

THE ICON – A GLIMPSE OF THE DIVINE

PRESENTATION OF ICON MOTIFS:

THE ICON – A GLIMPSE OF THE DIVINE

Like all other art, the art of the Orthodox Church developed within a particular culture and consequently may only be understood in the context of its own history. At the same time there is something timeless and universal about the icon. Its powerful mode of expression, which is both spiritual and aesthetic appeals to many people today. A more congenial ecumenical climate and the greater mobility enjoyed by most people has contributed to an increasing interest in the church traditions of other faiths. Many people of the Western world have come in contact with the art of icons when travelling to Orthodox countries such as Greece, Bulgaria, Romania and Russia. As well as representing a unique art experience, icons can also open the door to a spirituality that fulfils a deep, religious need.

The information society we live in produces a continuous stream of intrusive and rapidly changing visual stimuli. The mass media makes it possible for images to be devoured like consumer goods. And such a continuous, cursory stream of pictures has a disturbing effect on people's minds. Orthodox iconography has a form which inspires serenity and a content which invites meditation. The fact that icons are now, in our time, thought worthy of consideration is, not least, due to these contemplative qualities.

The word *icon* comes from the Greek *eikon,* meaning *image.* To separate art from other forms of pictorial art the Greeks use the word *agiografies– holy images* – when they speak about this special form of sacred art. All Orthodox art, irrespective of medium, is included in the icon concept; decorations executed on walls, such as mosaics and frescoes, reliefs in wood, metal or ivory, book illuminations, embroideries and enamel work. However, in English the word *icon* generally refers to a painting in the Orthodox tradition using egg tempera on a prepared wooden panel.

All the icons in this book belong to the latter category. They are based on authorised, mainly Greek and Russian, models and employ traditional motifs and techniques in their execution. The depiction of a new icon is not an uncompromising process of making an exact copy, but rather a process of re-creation in which the artist enters into a creative dialogue with the model. This type of modern icon painting which is marked by both the past and present may be classified as New Byzantinism.

THE TECHNIQUE OF ICON PAINTING

Painting an icon in accordance with Byzantine tradition is a painstaking and time consuming process which involves several different craft techniques. A well-seasoned, solid wood panel without knots and cracks is used as the base. Most of the icons presented in this book are painted on oak and beech, but pine, birch and plywood are also used. If an icon is to be more than 35-40 cm wide, several small planks must be glued together. Some need bracing with crossbars at the back to prevent warping. The front of the panel is gouged out leaving a surrounding frame and a shallow recessed surface for the motif. In the past this work was done with an axe and small plane, but today it is not unusual to use modern tools such as a band saw, horizontal routing machine and sanding machine.

First the wood is coated several times with animal glue size to make it less absorbent. Then the panel is covered with thin canvas and given a grounding of eight to ten coats of animal glue, white colour pigment and chalk. Before the grounding is applied, it is heated to ca 70°C. It is also an advantage to strain it to remove any coarse grains of sediment. The panel must dry, and if necessary be polished down between each coat. The plaster-like gesso forms an even and suitably absorbent base for the different layers of colour that will be applied. In some cases, if the surface structure is especially fine and the quality of the wood permits, the motif may be painted direct onto the wood. But first the surface must be grounded with animal glue.

The motif may be transferred to the panel using tracing paper, or sketched direct onto it with a pencil or tempera colour. An icon is always painted systematically – background to foreground.

Stage 1
This solid beech panel is in one piece and measures 31 x 41 cm. It is braced because of its width. The panel is 2.5 cm deep and has a border of 3.5 cm. The recessed surface is gouged out with a routing machine and polished smooth with sandpaper. The panel is then given two coats of glue size, made from one litre of water added to 75 grams of animal glue and heated to 70°C. Animal glue is obtainable as a powder or in wafers. Fish glue or gelatine may also be used for this purpose.

Stage 2
Here the panel has been covered with a piece of fine cotton cloth. The wood had already been given one coat of warm animal glue, and before this dried the cloth was dipped in glue and pressed onto the base. Air bubbles are removed by pressing the glue-soaked cotton on the surface using a circular movement of the fingers or a damp cloth. When the cotton is dry, the edges are cleanly cut with a scalpel. Then eight to ten coats of the grounding itself – a mixture of animal glue, chalk and titanium white colour pigment – is applied and polished to a smooth finish.

THE MYSTICAL LANGUAGE OF ICONS

When the outline is completed, the next step is to decide whether the background is to be painted or gilded. At times only the halo was gilded and the rest of the background covered with a colour that harmonised with the other colours.

The oldest and most demanding, but also most effective, gilding technique makes it possible to burnish the gold surface. To do this a special grounding containing clay and basalt is needed. This material, called bole, has a paste-like consistency. Bole mixed with animal glue is heated and applied to the area to be covered with gold leaf. Five to six coats of this grounding mixture are usually enough. This is then polished with steel wool, fine emery paper and agate stone until it is quite smooth. As even the tiniest dust particle or scratch will show when the extremely thin gold leaf is applied, the groundwork must be meticulously carried out. Bole has a red brown colour that shines through the gold and gives it a deep glow. The bole may also have a yellow ochre or black colour.

The gilding work itself requires special equipment. As well as the burnishing tools a gilding cushion of chamois leather, a gilding knife and a broad gilder's tip is needed to handle the gold leaf. Touching the gold leaf with the fingers makes it crumble and therefore it can only be handled indirectly. It is applied to the undercoating with a mixture of thinned animal glue and technical spirit and later lightly brushed with an acorn hair paintbrush to ensure that it is affixed. After a short time, dependent on room temperature, the gold may be polished with agate stone. To achieve a high lustre, the presssure used must be increased only gradually. In the Middle Ages the eyeteeth of wolves or bears were used as polishing tools.

Punching the halo breaks down the gilded surface and gives a special decorative effect.

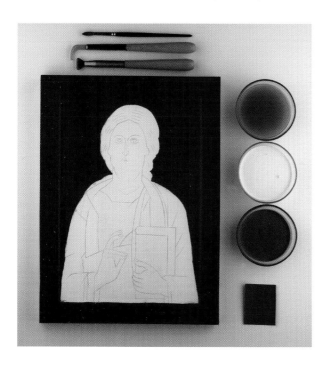

Stage 3

At this stage preparation of the panel is complete and it is ready to use. The intended motif – a Greek variant of Christ Pantocrator – was sketched in with pencil. As the icon is to be gilded, the background was covered with red brown bole; five to six coats were needed. This ground was then smoothed with sandpaper, polished with steel wool and the final finish done with agate. If the bole becomes too dry, it will no longer work. At this phase the time factor and the temperature of the room are crucial. Together with the animal glue, the ground will form a kind of cushion which will support the gold when it is burnished.

Stage 4

The gold (22 carat) is rolled out in thin wafers and may be bought as loose gold leaf or as transfer gold. A book of gold leaf contains 24 wafers measuring 9 x 9 cm. The loose gold leaf must be placed on a chamois leather cushion and cut with a special knife, then lifted with the help of static electricity using a broad gilder's tip. Transfer gold, pictured above, is easier to handle, because it lies on thin paper and may be cut with scissors. The gold is affixed to the undercoating with thinned animal glue and technical spirit. After a short time the gold may be brushed lightly with a round acorn hair paintbrush and burnished with agate.

Another simpler gilding technique entails affixing the gold with an oil-based, slow drying glue, but with this technique the gold cannot be burnished afterwards.

In accordance with century-old conventions icon painting is done with egg tempera. Colour pigments are mixed with a binding material made of egg yolk, water and vinegar. The resulting emulsion makes the colour half-transparent, and therefore several coats are needed to cover the white ground. As the underlying colour layer will shine through and affect the next layer, work must be done systematically so that the overlying colour is a lighter or darker shade of the previous coat. During the work process, the colours are mixed continually on a porcelain palette. Even the highlighting or shading of robes and skin is painted on a dark or half-dark base colour.

An icon may be painted using a relatively limited colour spectrum. The following colours form the basis:

Titanium white	*Light cadmium yellow*
Yellow ochre	*Chrome oxide green*
Burnt sienna	*Cobalt green*
Light cadmium red	*Ultramarine blue*
Dark cadmium red	*Cobalt blue*
Indian red	*Raw umbra*
Ivory black	*Burnt umbra*

Colour pigments have varying absorbent and covering abilities. Some are transparent, whereas others are opaque or half-opaque. Indian red, for example, will dominate black when mixed. These individual characteristics must be taken into consideration when working. As previously mentioned, modelling is carried out by a gradual building up from darker to lighter shades. The egg tempera technique is well suited to achieving

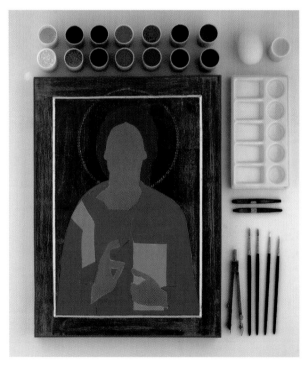

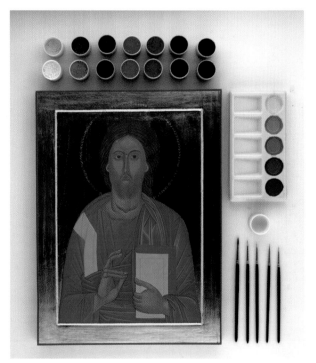

Stage 5

After the background is gilded and the halo punched, the base colour is applied. The emulsion is made of egg yolk and water (preferably distilled) mixed in the proportions 1:1. The emulsion can be made stronger or thinner, depending on the stage the work is at. A little vinegar keeps the egg fresh. The skin colour here is a combination of yellow ochre and burnt sienna, with a touch of oxide green and light cadmium red. The blue is ultramarine broken down with titanium white, ivory black, oxide green and yellow ochre. The red is light cadmium red broken down with titanium white and yellow ochre. In general no colour is unmixed.

Stage 6

The base colours form the basis for further building up of lighter and darker shades. The folds in the robes and the facial features – brow, eyes, nose, mouth and neck – are outlined with a thin paintbrush. These first, delicate contours function as aids delineating colour layers. To model the face and hands, a spectrum of dark, medium and light shades of the base colour are mixed on the palette. By systematically working from darker to lighter shades, a fine gradation from shaded areas to highlighted areas will appear. The drapery is built up in the same way.

THE MYSTICAL LANGUAGE OF ICONS

gradual transitions and fine details. Finally the contours are defined and the highlighting carried out. The contrast between light and dark areas may be further intensified by applying a dark glaze to the darkest colours.

Russian icons are somewhat different from Greek ones, both in style and in the manner the egg tempera medium is used. In the Russian tradition the wooden panel lies flat during painting so that many coats of unthinned base colour may be applied in a fluid state. This technique is reminiscent of water colour painting, especially in the early stage. Some areas of colour may be monochrome, something which is quite unusual in the Greek tradition. The icons of the Novgorod school are known for their distinctive luminous, transparent effect. The figures are light and elegant with an aura of spirituality. The icons of St George and Daniel in the Lions' Den (pp. 76 and 77) and The Fiery Ascent of the Prophet Elijah (p. 56) are based on models from the Novgorod school.

Within the different Greek schools, (for example the Macedonian and Cretan schools), much greater weight is placed on plasticity. The face, robes, scenery and architecture have bold contours and to some extent dramatic contrasts. The figures are clearly sculptured and combine energy and vitality. The panel does not lie flat during the work, but rests on an easel or at a 45° angle on a table. Surplus colour is removed before painting. The paintbrush also used is drier than in the Russian method, and the colour is applied in close, quick strokes. The round icon of Christ Pantocrator (p. 24) and The Baptism of Christ (p. 60) are based on models from the Cretan school.

The icons depicted in this book draw on both the Russian and the Greek traditions when it comes to painting technique and iconography.

Stage 7
The area which is to form the underlayer for the final highlight has been further defined. Correspondingly the shaded area has been made even darker with several thin layers of glazing. The lightest shade on the face will cover the middle of the forehead, the area just above the brow, the cheekbones, bridge of the nose, chin, ear lobes and certain areas of the neck. The deepest skin colour will be along the outer edge of the face and neck, along each side of the bridge of the nose, between the eyelid and brow, between the lower lip and throat and also as a base for the beard and moustache. The placing and size of the pupils of the eyes are decisive for the expression.

Stage 8
This step shows the completed icon. The inscriptions have been given the same colour as the border. The strictly stylised highlight is marked with thin, straight lines 1-2 mm apart. The highlight colour derives from mixing white in the lightest shade of its local colour. The brow, moustache and beard are painted with close, brown black lines on a golden brown ochre background. The varnish is to protect the surface and it also gives the painting a brighter lustre. In the old handbooks for icon painters there are many different recipes for varnish. Among the ingredients used are linseed oil, olive oil, resin, honey and beeswax.

BEAUTY AND TRUTH

The Byzantine Empire, with Constantinople as its political and religious centre, forms the historical background for the development of this special form of art. Constantinople – 'the second Rome' – was founded in 330 AD by Constantine the Great, the first Christian Emperor of the Roman Empire. After the Turkish invasion of the city in 1453, the Orthodox centre moved to Moscow – 'the third Rome'.

Russia's Christian inheritance came from Byzantium. The Nestor chronicle tells us how in 998 Prince Vladimir of Kiev chose Greek Orthodox Christianity as a unifying religion for his people from the reports about how beautiful the services were that the Greeks celebrated. Emissaries returned with impressions of different denominations, but after taking part in a service in Hagia Sofia, Constantinople, they were overwhelmed and spontaneously declared: *'We did not know whether we were in heaven or on earth. Such splendour and beauty are not found anywhere on earth: it is impossible to describe. We only know that God was there among the people.'* When nearly one thousand years later Dostoyevskij wrote: *'Beauty shall save the world,'* it was the outcome of a fundamental philosophical tenet that regards beauty and truth as one.

ART AND HOLY OBJECTS

The schematic and partly abstract use of form which distinguishes the art of icons, corresponds to certain formal tendencies in modern painting: namely simplification of composition, absence of naturalism and the illusion of space, and emphasis on line and surface. In such a way those who are interested in art and knowledgeable about modern art can assess iconography using purely aesthetic criteria. However, apart from any such outwardly formal features in common, the very character of icons is far removed from the assumptions that influence the production of a great deal of Western art.

The notion that a work shall represent something quite new, original and exceptional, reflects a view of art that idealises the subjective. This

opinion that has gradually become widespread lies behind the attitude that Orthodox iconography is repetitious and bound by tradition. A recurring question is therefore whether the icon painter may express anything of 'his own' in a work of art.

An icon painter living in the Middle Ages would not have understood such a question. He would probably have spent many years acquiring the style of a special school, and the range of motifs was more or less set beforehand. If he was connected to a workshop, the finished work would often be the result of a collective effort. Perhaps an apprentice had been given the task of applying the ground to the panel and grinding the colours. The Master himself gladly painted the most exacting parts such as the face, hands and feet, while he left the robes to a painter who had specialised in that work.

The icon is a holy object, the form being merely a receptacle for the content. And the content is determined by the Holy Scriptures and the Traditions of the Church. That is why the work process is marked more by discipline than by inspiration.

THE ICON'S STATUS AND FUNCTION

The icon is never complete in itself. It can never stand alone as an autonomous work of art, but refers to a spiritual dimension and forms part of a concrete, religious practice. As it expresses itself through a holy symbolic language, it cannot be read without a knowledge of Orthodox theology and spirituality.

An icon is *conventional* – it is rule-bound in both form and content. It is presented in a standardised form which builds on authorised models. Inasmuch as an icon shall pass on the official teachings of the Church, the painter is not free to incorporate his/her own subjective interpretations into the work. An icon is above the personal, it is an expression of the community's faith, a faith which is shaped within the *'the fellowship of the saints'*. Thus the icon painter is obliged to work in conformity with the authorised models. In order to call a painting an icon, it must have the characteristics of

Orthodoxy; it must express the true teachings in visual form, just as preaching is expressed verbally. (*Orto doxia* means *true teaching, true praise*.)

The Eastern Church tradition places words and images on an equal footing. The great theologian St John of Damascus (c. 675-749) points out that *'just as words encourage hearing, so do images stimulate the eyes'*. He regards words written in books as verbal icons. The text or speech expresses a mental picture. This fundamental equivalence between words and images, between theology and iconography leads implicitly to the forms being standardised. Both belief and a more precise definition of doctrine illustrate such standardisation. A characteristic feature of iconography is that form is depicted very consistently. With its specific rules for depiction, an icon is equivalent to language when it attempts to define dogmas as exactly as possible. But neither words nor pictures can give a completely satisfactory description of the substance of Christian faith. The mystery cannot be explained in forms created by humans. However, as conveyors of divine revelations, the Holy Scriptures and the Church Tradition impart spiritual truths. It is here that the icon appears as one of several mediums the Church uses to communicate the Gospel.

Because the icon has a teaching function, it has been given *canonical status*. This applies within the autocephalous Orthodox churches such as the Greek Orthodox and the Russian Orthodox. (*Autocephalous* means *independent, with own governing body*.) Among Catholics with Byzantine rites, for example the Greek Catholics in the Ukraine and the Melkites in the Middle East, sacred art has a similar formalised position.

The Western Catholic Church with Roman rites has an extremely varied practice regarding images. There were various reasons why the development in the Roman Catholic Church was so different from that of the Orthodox and Oriental churches. But here too we find instances where icons may have a prominent position as cult images. For the Poles, The Black Madonna in Czestochowa is the religious focal point of the nation.

At the 7th Ecumenical Council in Nicaea in 787 a century-long practice was given official approval. The council fathers recorded that *'The making of icons was not the creation of the painters, but an accepted institution and tradition within the universal Church... The idea and tradition came from the fathers, not from the painters. Only the art belongs to the painter, whereas the form without doubt comes from the fathers who founded the Church.'*

The icon has also a *dogmatic character* – it depicts visually that which the Church teaches verbally. A logical consequence of recognising the teaching authority an icon has, is that the painter is subject to church discipline. To ensure identification and continuity the same motif types have been handed down with remarkably small variations. Fixed iconographic patterns and work methods have gone from master to apprentice and gradually been compiled into painting handbooks. By faithfully recreating already established composition systems, icon painters have administered a unique spiritual inheritance that goes back to late Antiquity. Such a strict conservative practice has naturally had an effect on the development of motifs. At the same time the many distinctive schools and regional nuances bear witness to the fact that icon paintings have been modified by changing historical conditions and the artistry of the individual painter. A living tradition is not static, but contains a dynamic element. It is because of this that there is room within the icon tradition for further development within certain set limits.

The icon has a *liturgical function* – it constitutes an integral part of the life of a service in the Orthodox Church. In conformity with the Byzantine image programme, the interior of a church is decorated throughout with monumental frescoes or mosaics in the cupola, the arches and on the walls. The iconostasis, which separates the choir from the nave, is also decorated.

The impression given by a fully decorated iconostasis with its many rows of carefully planned motifs is overwhelming.

The liturgical environment of the church is unique, because it discloses a celestial reality that is revealed through the liturgical celebration. The Church recreates in the present what Christ and the saints said and did in the past. Praise, prayers, reciting the Gospel and the other holy texts and also partaking of the sacraments belong to a dimension of experience which constitutes *the liturgy*. An icon that depicts the actual feast or saint, is displayed and accessible for the veneration of the believers. According to St Basil the Great (329-379) *'the honour given to the image is transferred to its prototype'*. St Athanasius of Alexandria (295-373) expresses the same thought when he says *'The person who bows to an icon, bows to the king in it.'*

Among Orthodox Christians the icon also has a natural function as a private devotional image. It provides a reminder of what it portrays, a consciousness of the past in the present. In Russian homes the tradition is to place the house icon in the so-called 'beautiful corner' of the living room.

The icon is *didactic* – it illustrates and teaches about events and people in Bible and Church history. St John of Damascus was concerned that pictorial art should make it easier for those who could not read to understand the Christian message: *'What the book is to the literate, the image is to the illiterate.'* As well as mediating knowledge about belief an image may also stimulate feelings that lead to an inner arousal of belief. St John of Damascus refers to his own experience when he writes: *'I saw an icon depicting suffering, and I was unable to pass it without weeping, because what was happening was imparted to me as if it were real.'*

However, the icon is always more than an illustration with an educational goal. The icon is holy because of its subject matter – namely Christ himself. An image of God. Christ is the first perfect icon from whom the saints gather their radiance, and the man-made icon in its turn shall reflect this divine radiance.

ICONOCLASM AND THE TRIUMPH OF ORTHODOXY

The icon has been the subject of great discord. During the period of iconoclasm (resistance to images) from 726 to 843, confrontations took place between those who defended the then practice (the iconodules) and those who attacked the established use of images and who wished to eliminate all forms of figurative art (the iconoclasts). The cross could be accepted as a theological symbol, but not the person of Christ, the Mother of God or any saint.

The iconoclasts challenged the iconodules by asking how they could defend a practice which gave God a visible form. The iconoclasts with Leo III in the vanguard referred to the prohibition of images in the Old Testament. They maintained that displaying and using figurative art in connection with the Church was no better than idolatry. The use of images also conflicted with the Christian belief that God is perfect, transcendent and absolutely independent and sovereign over his own creation; neither does he let himself be known nor depicted. To give God a visible form was not permissible, it was even directly blasphemous, because it would diminish his majesty.

St John of Damascus agreed with this theological reasoning for not depicting God. He also agreed with his opponents that the Mosaic prohibition of images reflected an understanding of God which both Jews and Christians shared, and asked rhetorically: *'How can the invisible be depicted? How does one picture the inconceivable? How can one draw what is limitless, immeasurable, infinite? How can a form be given* to the formless? How does one paint the bodiless? How can you describe what is a mystery?'

Justification for the prohibition of images may also be found in God's transcendence and the danger of idolatry. St John of Damascus expounds his argument and recalls that God had no recognisable form before he manifested himself as Christ. But when the boundless, eternal, inaccessible and indescribable God became man, he could be depicted in an image. The mystery of the Incarnation is itself the crowning argument for the icon and legitimises the depiction of the divine. By following this argument consistently, St John could say: *'I have seen God in human form, and my soul was saved'*. He further says: *'In former times God, who is without form or body, could never be depicted. But now when God is seen in the flesh conversing with men, I make an image of the God whom I see. I do not worship matter; I worship the Creator of matter who became matter for my sake, who willed to take his abode in matter; who worked out my salvation through matter.'*

NICAEA II

Some years later, at the Ecumenical Council in Nicaea in 787, the so-called Nicaea II, the Council texts confirmed what St John of Damascus had already formulated in his defence tracts. The Church Council proclaimed that *'next to the sign of the precious and life-giving cross, venerable and holy icons – made of colours, pebbles, or any other material that is fitting – may be set in the holy churches of God, on holy utensils and vestments, on walls and boards, in houses and in streets. These may be icons of Our Lord and God the Saviour Jesus Christ, or of Our pure Lady the holy Theotokos, or of honourable angels, or of any saint. For the more these are kept in view through their iconographic representation, the more those who look at them are lifted up to remember and have an earnest desire for the prototypes. Also we declare that one may render to them the veneration of honour: not the true worship of our faith, which is due only to the divine nature, but the same kind of veneration as is offered to the form of the precious and life-giving cross, to the holy*

gospels and to the other holy items. Also we declare that one may honour these by bringing to them incense and light, as was the pious custom of the early Christians; for the honour to the icon, is conveyed to the prototype'.

This Council text defines icons as sacred objects of use with an edifying effect. Because God communicates through both words and images, it is legitimate to show the icons honour (*proskynesis*), whereas only God is worthy of worship (*latreia*). When the defenders of icons won their final victory over the iconoclasts at a Council in Constantinople in 843, they celebrated the victory with a special feast called 'The Triumph of Orthodoxy'. This liturgical feast is still celebrated on the first Sunday in Lent.

'The mystery of the Incarnation is itself a major argument for iconography and legitimises portrayal of the divine.'

THE INCARNATION AND THE ART OF THE ICON

The author of the Letter to the Hebrews sums up the main features in the history of salvation when he writes: *'Long ago God spoke to our ancestors in many and various ways by the prophets, but in these last days he has spoken to us through his Son, ... He is the reflection of God's glory, and the exact imprint of God's very being...'* (Heb 1, 1-3).

'The invisible Father is given a face through the Son.'

St John the Evangelist describes God's appearance through the Incarnation in a beautiful way: *'No one has ever seen God; the only Son who is in the bosom of the Father, he has made him known'* (Jn 1, 18). About himself Christ uses the following words: *'Whoever has seen me has seen the Father.'* (Jn 14, 9). St Paul expresses the same thought when he writes that *'He is the image (eikon) of the invisible God'* (Col 1,15).

An icon is always a copy (*mimesis*) of a model or prototype. According to Orthodox understanding of images, the model is present in an image by virtue of this likeness. Therefore an icon of Christ will mediate Christ's presence in a direct way. The image is of course not identical with the model – that would be to confuse the symbol with what it symbolises. The icon is a symbol which represents a reality outside the actual image. At the same time, in a certain sense, the symbol is a part of the prototype through its likeness (*homoioma*). St Theodore the Studite, who argued against the iconoclasts in the 800s, explains this relationship with a metaphor: The portrait (the type) is associated with the model (the prototype) like a print is to a seal and a shadow to a figure. They resemble each other, but exist in quite different forms. However, if the icon is only interesting in itself, it loses its symbolic function and is reduced to an aesthetic object without any mediating power.

When Moses asked to see God's splendour, he was told: *'You cannot see my face; for no one shall see me and live'* (Ex 33, 20). God's inner being or essence (*ousia*) is absolutely inaccessible to men. When God communicates with the help of speech or other supernatural, discernible phenomena in Old Testament times, it is as an example that he makes himself indirectly known through his powers or energies (*dynamis*).

As we have seen, the Mosaic prohibition against images builds on God's absolute transcendence. But as God voluntarily allows himself to be limited by time and space, unites with matter and becomes flesh, man and all of creation is led into a completely new, existential situation. God makes himself accessible and discernible. The person of Christ is the revealed form (*hypostasis*) of God. The invisible Father has a face in the Son. Man can now hear, see and touch the incarnated Word with his hands and consequently form an image of him (1 Jn 1,1).

As a result of the Incarnation, matter has become able to carry the divine within itself. Painting an icon may be seen as a reflection of the same process. The icon bears witness to a mystical interaction between the Creator and creation: Through Christ's descent to earth, God took part in human nature, so that man could take part in divine nature (2 Pet 1, 4). The Incarnation gives matter a holy capacity which points towards the perfect existence in the new world. It is this re-created, illuminated creation which constitutes the fundamental theme of the icon. The icon is a piece of transformed matter with a sacramental character – a physical sign of a divine presence. During its production it has undergone a change. In this way the icon's sacramental materiality may be a reminder of the change towards greater likeness with God (*theosis*) that marks the saints.

RANGE OF MOTIFS

In principle the icon painter's repertoire consists of the complete gallery of persons in the New and Old Testaments, as well as holy men and women in the Church tradition. A motif may incorporate one person, a group, an event or the progress of an event.

According to Dionysius the Areopagite (c. 500), a Christian philosopher of Late Antiquity, the spiritual and material world is arranged in a hierarchical system. He sees cosmos divided into three different spheres. In the upper sphere is the Holy Trinity: the Father, Son and Holy Spirit. Then comes the hierarchy of angels: seraphim, cherubim, thrones, dominions, virtues, powers, principalities, archangels and angels. Finally there is the ecclesiastical hierarchy: baptism, the Eucharist, confirmation, bishops, priests, deacons, monks, lay people and catechumens. This way of structuring the world is quite apparent in the motif repertoire of Orthodox iconography.

Dionysius the Areopagite combines Jewish-Christian creation beliefs with Neoplatonic teaching to explain the relationship between the Creator and the created. The notion that all of creation is illuminated with a divine light is an important part of the basic concept regarding iconography. The ability to reflect this light is dependent on the distance to the source.

The Trinity may be portrayed indirectly with reference to the three men who visited Abraham in a grove at Mamre (Gen 18). This motif is also called *The Hospitality of Abraham*. As the Father and the Holy Spirit were not incarnated, they can only be portrayed with the help of symbolic indications, for example a hand and a dove. *The Hospitality of Abraham* is the only motif in Orthodox iconography where all the persons of the Deity are given human form. Another much discussed portrayal of The Trinity shows the Father, *'an ancient one'* (Dan 7, 9), sitting on a throne. The Son sits on the Father's lap holding a dove in his hands.

Of the icons of Christ, *Christ Pantocrator, Christ Immanuel* and *The icon not created by human hands (Acheiropóietos)* are most depicted. Of the angels: the seraphim, cherubim and archangels are among the best known. Icons of the Mother of God with Child are found in a great many variations. The most important types here are *Our Lady of the Sign, (Blachernitissa), The Mother of God, Hodegetria* (She who Shows the Way) and *The Mother of God, Eloeusa* (Tenderness).

The feast day or festival icons represent a separate group of motifs which correspond with the most important liturgical feasts of the Church year. Of these, twelve compose a sequence from the life of Jesus and are in the following order:

1. *The Annunciation*
2. *The Nativity of Christ*
3. *The Presentation in the Temple*
4. *The Baptism of Christ*
5. *The Raising of Lazarus*
6. *The Transfiguration*
7. *The Entry into Jerusalem*
8. *The Crucifixion*
9. *The Descent into Hell*
10. *The Ascension*
11. *Pentecost*
12. *The Dormition of The Mother of God*

The saint icons include such diverse groups as the patriarchs, prophets, evangelists, apostles, martyrs, holy mothers and virgins, holy hermits, monks, nuns and founders of monasteries, theologians, spiritual supervisors, holy bishops, priests and deacons. In addition to these are the lay people with the statues of saints.

THE CHURCH AS MICROCOSM

In accordance with Orthodox teaching about the Church, the interior of the church itself is regarded as a three dimensional icon. The church is a model of the universe, a vision of the redeemed, transformed cosmos, an architectonic *mimesis* of a divinely ordered universe. The Greek word *mimesis* means a *reminder* or *copy of*. The interior of the church is a reminder of God's constant and visible revelation in the history of mankind, at the same time as it is a copy, in the sense that it symbolises God's perfect kingdom 'up there'. The Lord's house is heaven on earth. The Scriptures tell of the Lord's house as a place chosen for prayer. The faithful who

'In the cupola reigns Christ Pantocrator'

worship God within the framework of the earthly liturgy, reflect the divine liturgy which takes place before God's throne on high. In this way the liturgy celebrated by the Church on earth is an image – an icon – of the liturgy the saints celebrate in heaven.

With certain adjustments, Dionysius the Areopagite's splendid model of cosmos is reflected in the manner in which a Byzantine church is decorated. The set scheme of decoration outlined here was first given its final form in the post-iconoclastic era. That is from the middle of the 9th century and onwards. But the theoretical basis for this decorative programme was also fixed many centuries earlier. The notion that a church is a microcosm becomes strikingly obvious when we study the Byzantine cross cupola church. As the name implies, the main structure of the ground plan is in the form of a cross with a dome that arches over the crossing point. The cross symbolises Christ's cross as well as the four points of the compass, whereas the cupola symbolises the sphere of heaven. In this way we see that the whole cosmos is encompassed by Christ's redeeming death on the cross.

The decorative programme is arranged in a strictly hierarchical manner, from the top of the cupola down to the floor. In the cupola Christ Pantocrator is enthroned – the All-ruler – the almighty Creator, Saviour and Judge. He is framed in a medallion and portrayed frontally as a half figure. The physical placement, the frontality and eye contact contribute to heightening the impression of a majestic presence.

This central figure of Christ Pantocrator is often framed by a circular rainbow supported by angels. In the dome itself we find prophets from the Old Testament who foresaw the coming of the Saviour King, the Messiah, while the four corners supporting the cupola are reserved for the evangelists who described God's visible coming in the form of man. The prophets proclaimed the promises, the evangelists were the witnesses to their fulfilment.

At the very top of the walls a motif sequence has been designed to contain the twelve scenes previously mentioned from the life of Jesus. Below the motif sequence is a splendid place for different portrayals of the saints, often those connected with local traditions. The figurative decoration stops at shoulder height so that the congregation constitutes the next step in a hierarchically arranged microcosm. At the very bottom, harmonious flowing drapery is often painted, or decorative marble plates are inset in the wall. In this way it is possible for a person of our time to enter the church and gain the experience of being an integrated part of the divine drama that the iconography expresses. Since man is made in the image of God, he himself is an icon and part of the complete decoration.

The choir is the liturgical centre of the body of the church and is reserved for the clergy serving at the altar. The celebrating priest appears as an icon of the high priest, Christ himself – the main celebrant in the divine liturgy. The visual presentation of this thought is found just above the altar in the apse in a portrayal of Christ distributing bread and wine to the apostles.

The faithful on earth may partake in the heavenly liturgy because of God's descent into matter through the birth of Jesus – the mystery of the Incarnation. The uniting of heaven and earth, of God and man, is manifested through the placing of Mary, the Mother of God, above the portrayal of Christ celebrating the Eucharist just mentioned. Mary is depicted frontally, often with her hands lifted in prayer and with the Child Jesus on her lap, or framed in a circle on

     THE MYSTICAL LANGUAGE OF ICONS

her breast. By being a bodily channel for God's coming, Mary may be likened to a ladder that joins heaven and earth. No person has been as close to God as Mary was. The King of Heaven descended into Mary's womb, allowed himself to be born and to take his seat on Mary's lap.

By placing that motif directly above the altar, the connection between the Incarnation and the sacramental continuance of the Incarnation through the Eucharist is made clear. The altar symbolises the heavenly throne and Christ's grave and therefore actualises the whole scope of the redemption drama. Thus we can follow the divine descent from the heavenly throne via Mary's womb and lap and down to Christ's grave. The descent is shown visually with the help of the icon and communicated sacramentally in the partaking of the body and blood of Jesus Christ.

PREFIGURATION AND HIERARCHICAL MODEL

The church is prefigured in the Old Testament in Noah's Ark, the Tabernacle in the desert and Solomon's temple in Jerusalem. The tabernacle and temple were divided horizontally into the most holy, the holy, and the forecourt. This ground plan is reflected in the church building with the choir, the nave and narthex (or entrance hall). The building has an east-west orientation, with the choir facing east towards the garden of Eden, the lost paradise. The church is expecting Jesus Christ, the Sun of Righteousness, to return from the east. Cosmologically the choir stands for the divine world and anthropologically for the spirit of man. Cosmologically the nave represents the redeemed world and anthropologically the human body. The choir enlightens and leads the nave just as the human spirit guides and influences the body. According to this model the narthex corresponds to the underworld, the world in everlasting darkness. It is there the unredeemed dwell, captives of the fall of man.

We can also identify a hierarchical structure along the vertical and horizontal axes in the interior of the church. Just as the most holy in the temple was reserved for the high priest, the holy was intended for believing Jews and the fore-

court for the unclean and heathen, so the clergy in the church have their place in the choir, the lay people in the nave and those preparing for baptism are assigned to the entrance hall.

CELEBRATION AND EXPECTATION

So far we have seen the decorative programme in relation to space, but it may also be interpreted along a time axis. The motifs from the eras of the Old and New Testaments, as well as the church history that followed, refer to relevant salvation events that may be associated with a certain time and place. During the annual cycle of the church calendar this historic-mythological past is made liturgically simultaneous for the devout. The Church actualises the gospel by retelling it. The service constitutes a liturgical-sacramental presence in which events of the past are made applicable to the here and now. The liturgy may be explained as a drama representing Christ's acts of redemption. The different feasts take, so to speak, events out of the Holy Scriptures and motifs down from the walls.

The Church celebrates something which has happened and looks forward to something that will happen. The expectation that Christ will come again and re-establish all of creation, the terrifying fear of the end of the world and the Last Judgement as described in the gospels and St John's apocalyptic visions, have their place on the west wall of the nave. The realisation of these events will bring church history to a close and introduce a new era where creation regains its lost glory, a glory the Church carries within itself by being a prefiguration of the coming world, the 'New Jerusalem'.

CHARACTERISTICS OF FORM

With the help of certain formal means the icon painter portrays people who appear in a holy state. This holy state is symbolised by the halo surrounding the head, and in all icons we find the face is a major focal point. An icon is not limited to portraying just a surface similarity of its subject, but attempts primarily to express inner, spiritual qualities which radiate from the whole person, especially the face. Frontality and eye contact indicate closeness and concentrated attention. To be completely present in something is a divine characteristic which marks the saints. Therefore a face is seldom depicted in profile; an exception may be Judas kissing Jesus in Gethsemane. He is already half turned away and has lost his halo.

It is not the aim of the iconographer to portray correctly the anatomy of the human body. The drawing of the figure is entirely schematic and stylised, and features such as an elongated, ascetic body, large eyes, and a small nose and mouth show that the person portrayed belongs to another dimension.

Drapery is clearly ornamented with defined

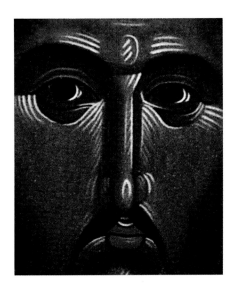

contours and parts are marked with highlighting. The folds in the robes, however, correspond to a large degree to the posture of the model. Some of the colours have a certain symbolic meaning, while others have a purely decorative function.

Elements such as the surroundings and architecture, which contribute to the environment, function as scenery for the person or event, and a building is often seen from different angles at the same time. This *inconsistent perspective* gives the elements a flat quality and counteracts the illusion of depth. The object is not to create a realistic impression; on the contrary, it is to lead the thoughts towards an existence that is 'without end'. To show that the icon refers to

a transcendent dimension, *inverse perspective* is used. This is done by making the objects farthest away the largest and the closest ones smallest. Following this principle, a rectangular footstool would be depicted as smaller at the front than at the back. The sloping lines on each side (the orthogonals) do not converge towards a vanishing point on the surface of the icon as they do in a naturalistic painting, but diverge into infinite space 'behind' the motif. If we follow the lines in the opposite direction, we find that they meet at the spectator. It is as if the spectator is being looked at by the person in the portrait (see discussion of the icon on page 29).

Another special feature of icons is that when compared to the surroundings the main figure is often strikingly large. This is called *hierarchical perspective*. For example, a motif of The Nativity shows Mary resting on a covering in the centre of the painting while the Child Jesus, who appears unnaturally large for a newly-born baby, lies in a crib painted in inverse perspective. The other people in the composition – Joseph, the shepherds and the women who washed Jesus – are secondary and accordingly relatively small compared to the Mother of God and the Child Jesus (see discussion of the icon on page 41).

Light is presented in a manner that underlines the supernatural character of the icon. It radiates from the motif itself, and not, as is the case in a realistic painting, from a conjectured exterior source of light. Of course there is no sharply outlined shadow on the icon, only a certain degree of object shadow. The face, robes, hills and buildings are modelled by giving them lighter or darker shades of the local colour. It is the gold leaf in particular which gives the impression that the icon is luminous. In addition, the highlighted parts on the face and robes, the landscape and buildings show that the motif is not lighted from a certain angle, but completely surrounded and permeated with light. The matter is no longer solid, but permeable and transparent, with the ability to reflect the rays from a divine source of light. Those who are well acquainted with Orthodox iconography will often be able to identify a saint by the robes, gestures and fixed attributes, but as well as such recognisable features, an icon will also have a text. The icon is not complete – or legitimate as a holy image – before the name of the motif has been written on it. The inscription identifies the motif and also expresses the close association between name and person; between word and image. To mark the historic origin of a model, most inscriptions in this book are given in Greek or Old Church Slavonic, but considering the universal character of the Church, there is nothing to hinder the use of English in titles.

The custom of taking a newly-painted icon to the church to have it blessed expresses a wish to mark the icon's sacramental character. Through a conscious action centred on God, which for example allows the icon to lie on the altar during the celebration of the Eucharist, the icon's power to act as a medium for a holy presence is confirmed for the owner.

As we have seen, the icon's motif is based on a historic event through which God has manifested himself (a so-called *theophany*). However, in as far as the motif has a current interest over and above the historic event, a style is used which underlines its universality and timelessness. As an expression of divine revelation the icon is subject to neither the laws of nature nor the reason of man. The icon is thus no illusion of the physical, visible world, but a vision of the spiritual, invisible world.

Perspective

Detail of icon page 36:

The crib in which the Child Jesus lies is shown in inverse perspective. It is seen from above, whereas the rest of the motif is seen frontally. In relation to the secondary persons in this icon (Joseph, the shepherds and the women who washed the child) the newly-born baby appears noticeably large. Size according to rank (hierarchical perspective) is much used in iconography. This leads to attention being focused on the important elements in the picture. Seen in relation to Mary, the child has a more natural size. However, Mary dominates the composition.

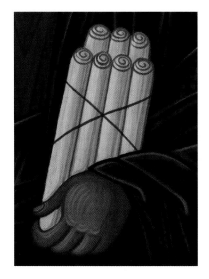

Attribute

Detail of icon on page 67:

The hand holding a bundle of scrolls is that of the apostle Paul, probably carrying his own letters. In addition to the inscriptions and recognisable physiognomy, a person may also be identified by an attribute. This is a fixed feature which says something about the person. In Western Church art the apostles are often depicted with the device that led to their death and martyrdom. As St Paul was beheaded, his attribute is a sword. In icons the apostles most often hold a book.

Symbol

Detail of icon page 62:

Inasmuch as the icon tradition did not permit a direct portrayal of God the Father, God's help or intervention was often symbolised by a hand introduced into the picture from above. Divine revelation – for example in connection with the Baptism of Jesus and The Transfiguration – is expressed as concentric circles sending out rays of light. The icon of St George and the Dragon combines these two symbols. The inviting hand may be identified as Christ's from the inscription IC–XC.

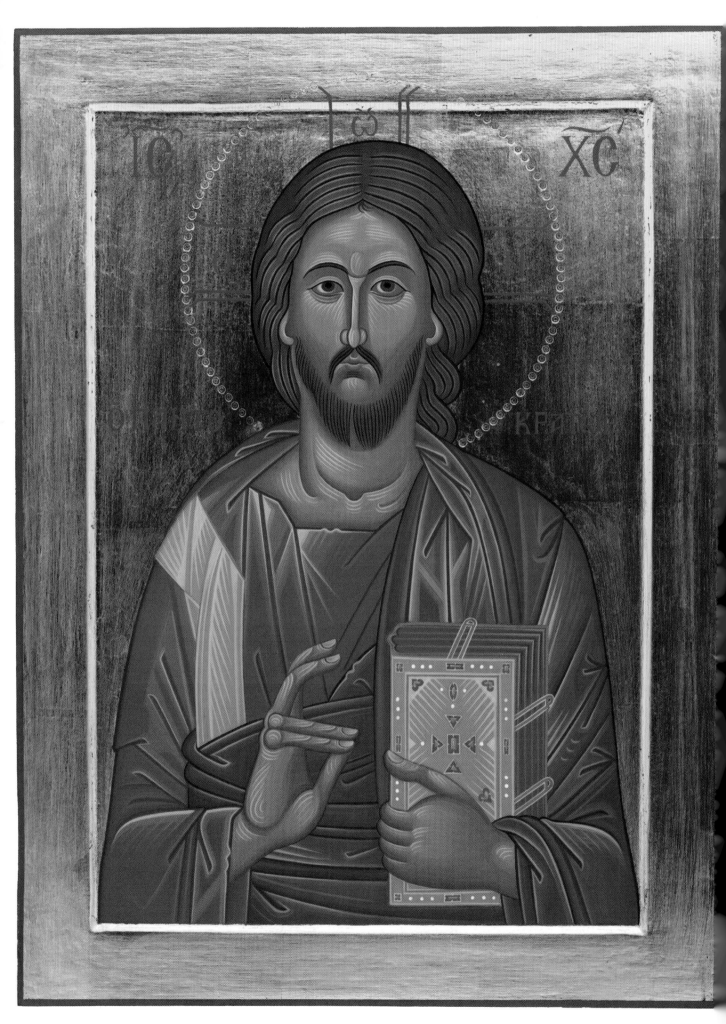

Christ Pantocrator

Greek variant. Cretan school. Egg tempera on oak. 31 x 42 cm (1998)

PRESENTATION OF ICON MOTIFS

Christ Pantocrator

Serbian variant
Egg tempera on oak. 27 x 35 cm (1997)

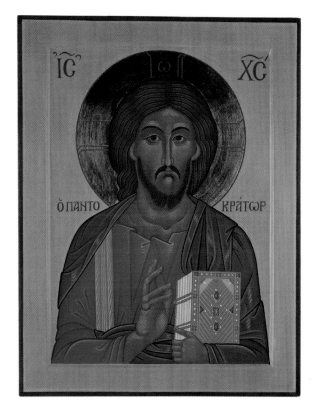

Christ Pantocrator (The All-ruler) is an icon of the Creator, the Saviour and the Judge. Here he is portrayed frontally as a half figure. The face is authoritative, but also gentle, the eyes are wide open looking directly at us. The two-piece robe he is wearing, a red tunic *(chiton)* and a blue cape *(himation)*, symbolises the two natures of Christ: the divine and the human. The broad band over the right shoulder, a so-called *clavus*, is a remnant from the Roman imperial court which indicates high official status. Christ's right hand is raised in blessing, while he holds the book of the Gospels in his left one.

The halo surrounding his head is a well-known symbol which denotes a sanctified state. The Greek letters ὁ ὤν inscribed on the arms of the cross are the present tense of the verb *to be*, and may be translated as *the abiding one* or *the one who is*. The perfect, indescribable and absolutely transcendent God, who presented himself to Moses as *'I am who I am'* (Ex 3,14), is, so to say, invisibly present behind the Son by virtue of his own name. The initials IC – XC are the first and last letters of Jesus Christ.

The sign of the blessing may be interpreted as a dogmatic statement; the joining of the three fingers refers to the Holy Trinity, whereas the two that are crossed symbolise the two natures of Christ and his death on the cross.

According to Orthodox tradition, an icon shall be honoured, because it manifests and actualises the spiritual reality towards which the faithful turn. In this way an icon may be a reminder of God's presence and an aid in prayer. Characteristics such as frontality and eye contact emphasise the *I – thou* relationship.

The use of gold leaf is an important aesthetic agent in the art of icons, but it is also a symbol with a specific theological significance. The gold symbolises what is known as *'the uncreated light'*. The uncreated light stands in contrast to the created light, for example sunlight, lamplight or candlelight which all have the quality of lighting an object, which again casts a shadow.

On an icon the outer, created light sources are subordinate to the uncreated light which expresses a fundamental quality of God's nature. Nobody has created the Creator; in other words God is *uncreated*. God is the only one who exists by virtue of himself. Everything else exists because it is created. Only of the Son is it said that *'he is born, not created, in the likeness of the Father'* (from the Nicene Creed).

The Scriptures say of God that *'It is he alone who... dwells in unapproachable light'* (1 Tim 6, 16) and that *'God is light'* (1 Jn 1, 5). Christ speaks of himself as *'the light of the world'* (Jn 8, 12). All who come near God are illuminated and transformed by the uncreated light. The holy persons portrayed on an icon are illuminated from the inside and made translucent because their light comes from God himself. As light is thought to 'slip through' matter, the phenomenon of cast shadows is unknown. This idea may also be transferred to the painting technique it-self. Egg tempera colour is partly transparent, so that each layer of colour has an effect on the next layer. In this manner light penetrates through the colour physically as well.

All theological reflection on the art of the icon has its origin in that *'God created man in his image – in his icon'* (Gen 1, 26). However, because of the fall, a disintegration of man occurred and the divine image was tarnished. The divine image was not lost, but enveloped in darkness. According to this metaphor, the person who surrenders to sin may be said to allow layers of soot to darken the icon, so that it loses its radiance and vitality. For God, the image was reinstated through the life of Jesus Christ, his sacrificial death and resurrection. Redeemed man, for his part, is called upon to realise his likeness with God – to become a living icon. In Greek this lifelong process is called *theosis* (deification). A transformation into greater likeness with God gives the icon back its splendour.

Christt Pantocrator

Left:
Round, Greek variant. Cretan school.
Model: fresco from the Monastery of Kaisariani, Greece.
Egg tempera on turned beech. 68 cm diameter (1989)

Right:
Standing, Greek variant.
Egg tempera on driftwood. 17 x 95 cm (1993)

It is this light that radiates from the faces of the saints.

The Greek word *Pantokrator* is used in several places in The Revelation of St John. In two of the quotes, we find both the verb form ὁ ὢΝ – *the abiding* or *the one who is* (used as an inscription of the cross halo), and the name *Pantocrator* – translated as *The Ruler of All* or *The Almighty* (the title of the icon):

'"*I am the Alpha and Omega*",
says the Lord God,
*who is (*ὁ ὢΝ *– the one who is)*
and who was
and who is to come,
the Almighty (Pantocrator)' (Rev 1, 8).

'*Holy, holy, holy,*
the Lord God the Almighty (Pantocrator),
*who was and is (*ὁ ὢΝ *– the one who is)*
and is to come' (Rev 4, 8).

Triptych with Deesis

Greek variant. Cretan school. Egg tempera on wood. 61 x 49 cm (1989)

A triptych is a set of three, hinged paintings which may be opened and closed like a cupboard. On this triptych Christ Pantocrator is flanked by the Mother of God and John the Baptist, or the 'Forerunner' as he has been called in the Eastern Church. Both are turned towards Christ with their hands raised in prayer. The text in the open book is taken from John 8, 12: *'I am the light of the world. Whoever follows me will never walk in darkness, but will have the light of life'*. As well as Christ speaking about himself as the light, the symbolism of light is further emphasised by the gilded background. Christ is the light and is surrounded by light, and all the saints radiate this divine light.

According to old Church Tradition, it was intended that Mary and John should have a special assignment and act as intercessors for mankind, which is why they are found by Christ's throne and future judgement seat in heaven. This position indicates how close they were to Christ during his earthly life. No-one was as close to God's Son as Mary, who carried him under her heart. Jesus gave John the following unusual tribute: *'Truly, I tell you, among those born of women no one has arisen greater than John the Baptist'* (Mt 11, 11).

A three figure group such as the above constitutes a central motif on an iconostasis, the picture screen which marks the transition between the nave and the sanctuary. The Greek word *deesis* means *intercession*. On the iconostasis, the row of intercessors is usually extended with the archangels Michael and Gabriel, the apostles Peter and Paul, the Church fathers Basil the Great and John Chrysostom and other saints.

THE MYSTICAL LANGUAGE OF ICONS

King and High Priest

Greek variant. Egg tempera on beech. Guilded silver work on frame. 29.5 x 35 cm (1999)

In this icon Christ is depicted as a representative of officialdom; he is both King and High Priest. An Orthodox bishop wears similar liturgical robes when he celebrates a service. Over the *sakkos* (a tunic with wide sleeves decorated with small crosses) the bishop wears a broad white stole of wool or silk *(omoforion)* which is similar to the stole used in Latin ritual. When this icon is placed on the back of a bishop's throne, his high official function becomes clear. The Christian king, the bishop and the priest get their mandates from Christ himself.

The texts in the open book refer to Christ's kingdom and the words used to introduce the sacrament of the Eucharist; *'My kingdom is not from this world.'* (Jn 18, 36), and *'Take eat; this is my body... for this is my blood of the covenant, which is poured out for many for the forgiveness of sins'* (Mt 26, 26-28).

In the Letter to the Hebrews the story of the Old Testament king and priest Melchizedek is explained as a prefiguration, a symbolic model, of Christ. The pre-existence of Christ as well as his divine status and priestly office are foreshadowed in this remote figure: *'Without father, without mother, without genealogy, having neither beginning of days nor end of life, but resembling the Son of God, he remains a priest for ever'* (Heb 7, 3).

Further it is said that *'... we have such a high priest, one who is seated at the right hand of the throne of the Majesty in the heavens, a minister in the sanctuary and true tent that the Lord, and not any mortal has set up'* (Heb 8, 1-2). The perfect, divine liturgy, where Christ is the priest, may be interpreted as a model for its earthly counterpart.

The title of this icon refers to a prophecy by Isaiah: *'Therefore the Lord himself will give you a sign. Behold a young woman shall conceive and bear a son, and shall call his name Immanuel.'* (Is 7, 14). The subject is the pre-existing Christ (who has always existed) and the incarnated Christ (who became man). The cross indicates Christ's future as our Saviour.

The icon shows a beardless young man, but at the same time his age is indeterminate, because he emanates the wisdom of an old man. The twelve-year-old Jesus aroused amazement among the learned in the temple (Lk 2, 46-47). In Greek such a mature young person is called *paidariogeron – an old child.*

In addition to the prophecy by Isaiah, this particular motif may also be associated with a vision the prophet Daniel tells us about: *'I saw one like a human being coming with the clouds of heaven. And he came to the Ancient One and was presented before him. To him was given dominion and glory and kingship, that all peoples, nations, and languages should serve him. His dominion is an everlasting dominion that shall not pass away, and his kingship is one that shall never be destroyed'* (Dan 7, 13-14).

During the hearing by the High Council, Christ interprets this text literally when he says: *'From now on you will see the Son of Man seated at the right hand of Power and coming on the clouds of heaven'* (Mt 26, 64).

Christ Immanuel

Left:
Greek variant, Macedonian school.
Egg tempera on pine.
Text: Jn 8, 12. Diameter 43 cm (1988)

Right:
Model: mosaic from San Marco, Venice.
Egg tempera on wood with glass beads.
26.5 x 52 cm (1991)

This version of *Christ Immanuel* is somewhat similar to the *Pantocrator* type in as much as the right hand is raised in blessing and the left one is holding a scroll. The scroll symbolises both the Gospel and Logos – the Word which became man. The stars, flowers and grass bring to mind creation and Logos as a creating principle: *'All things came into being through him and without him not one thing came into being'* (Jn 1, 3). St Paul writes of Christ that *'he became for us wisdom from God'* (1 Cor 1, 30). When Solomon talks about Wisdom as a person who took an active part in creating the universe, it seems natural to identify Wisdom as the young, playful, pre-existent Christ: *'When he established the heavens, I was there, when he drew a circle on the face of the deep... then I was beside him, like a master worker, and I was daily his delight rejoicing before him always, rejoicing in his inhabited world and delighting in human nature'* (Pro 8, 27 and 30-31).

The footstool is painted in inverse perspective. The diverging lines have their vanishing point in front of the surface of the picture, with the spectator, and not at a point on the surface of the picture as we find when central perspective is used. *Christ Immanuel* is the actual subject who comes to meet the spectator. The frontal posture of the body and the eye contact emphasise the relationship between the viewer and the one viewed.

Christ Enthroned

Greek variant, after
Emmanuel Tzanes
of Crete (1664)
Egg tempera on oak.
Burnished gold.
24 x 45 cm (1989)

The evangelists describe Christ as being all-mighty and humble, authoritative yet merciful. Gabriel says to Mary of the coming Saviour that *'He will be great, and called the Son of the Most High'* (Lk 1, 32). St Paul addresses Christ as *'... he who is the blessed and only Sovereign, the King of Kings and Lord of lords'* (1 Tim 6, 15). He calls himself *'servant'* and *'Son of Man'*.

The immense diversity in the person of Christ may also be read from this icon. Christ radiates a gentle authority which inspires awe and attraction at the same time. The icon presents the triumphant Sovereign of heaven and the future Judge the Church worships and awaits: *'He shall come in all his glory to judge the living and the dead, whose kingdom shall have no end'* (from the Nicene Creed).

The quotation in the open book gives a new dimension to the otherwise conventional icono-graphy of rulership, because it reveals Christ's sympathetic disposition: *'Come to me all you that are weary and are carrying heavy burdens, and I will give you rest. Take my yoke upon you, and learn from me; for I am gentle and humble in heart and you will find rest for your souls.'* (Mt 11, 28-29).

After fulfilling God's will on earth, the Son again took his seat *'at the Father's right hand'*. He returned to his place beside the Father taking with him his human nature in which he had clad himself at the Incarnation. St John of Damascus formulates the mystery thus: *'Through him, human nature arose from the deepest depths to the highest heights, and in him is seated on the Father's throne.'*

THE MYSTICAL LANGUAGE OF ICONS

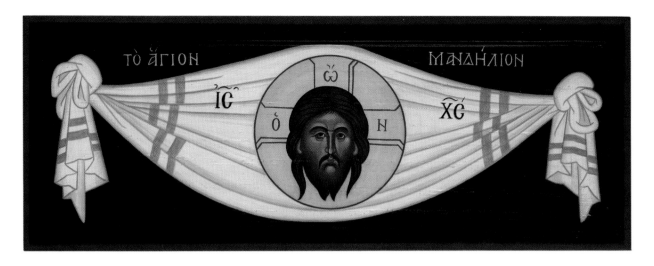

'God's only begotten Son shows us
his Father's beauty by presenting
himself in his radiant image.
First and foremost we see
the Son with the eyes of the heart,
but also with our human eyes,
for he bent down and came down
to us.'

Cyril of Alexandria

Mandylion

Above:
Greek variant.
Model: fresco from Studenica
Monastery, Serbia.
Egg tempera on oak.
Dark blue background.
12 x 32 cm (1997)

Left centre:
Russian variant. Novgorod school.
Egg tempera on beech.
Burnished gold with punching.
19.5 x 25.5 cm (1993)

Right centre:
Russian variant. Novgorod school.
Egg tempera on beech.
Blue background.
22 x 27 cm (1994)

Below:
Russian variant.
Egg tempera on beech.
Brown background.
15.5 x 22 cm (1995)

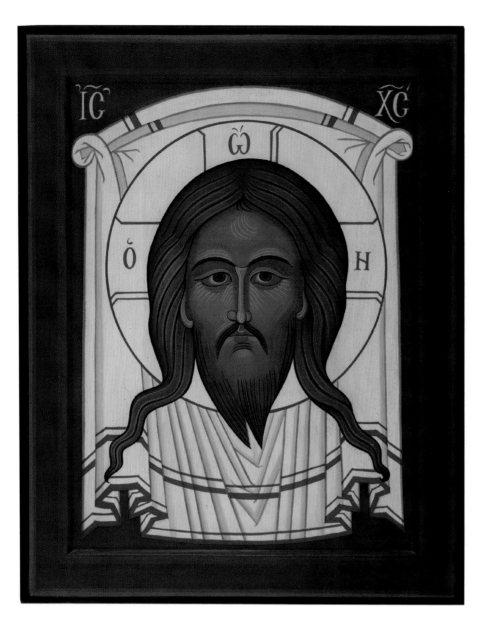

Mandylion

Left:
Russian variant.
Novgorod school.
Egg tempera on beech.
22 x 27 cm (1994)

Right:
Greek variant.
Egg tempera on wood
with papyrus surface.
13 x 18 cm (1997)

The word *mandylion* is Greek and means *cloth.* When this word is used as the title of an icon, it refers to a motif where the face of Christ is portrayed on a cloth. This motif is often called *The icon not created by human hands*, in Greek *Acheiropóietos*. In the Russian tradition it is called *Christ with the wet beard.*

The legend is about a certain king Abgarus who lived in Edessa. King Abgarus suffered from a skin complaint, probably leprosy. He heard that the prophet Jesus had healed many sick people. Could he perhaps also cure the king? With this hope as a motivating force he sent his servant Ananias with a letter inviting Jesus to Edessa. Ananias arrived at the place where Jesus was, but could not get near enough to meet him because of the huge crowd. Ananias did not wish to return empty-handed to his master so he climbed onto a high rock and tried to draw a picture of Jesus, but found he could not reproduce his features, because of the radiance shining from his face. However, Jesus noticed him and called him to his side. He told Ananias that he was unable to travel to Edessa, but later one of his disciples would visit the king. He then asked for a cloth and a basin of water, wrung out the cloth and covered his face with it. It was thus that the miraculous impression of the holy face became transferred to the cloth – an image 'not made by human hands'. Ananias took the cloth back to Edessa with him where it became the holiest relic – a divine sign with healing power.

The church historian Eusebius (2nd century) renders the following letters thus, supposedly exchanged between King Abgar and Jesus:

THE MYSTICAL LANGUAGE OF ICONS

THE EPISTLES OF JESUS CHRIST AND ABGARUS, KING OF EDESSA

CHAPTER 1

A copy of the letter written by King Abgarus to Jesus and sent to him by Ananais, his footman, to Jerusalem, inviting him to Edessa.

1 *Abgarus, King of Edessa, to Jesus the good Saviour, who appears at Jerusalem, greetings. 2 I have been informed concerning you and your cures, which are performed without the use of medicines and herbs. 3 For it is reported, that you cause the blind to see, the lame to walk, do both cleanse lepers and cast out unclean spirits and devils, and restore them to health who have been long diseased, and raisest up from the dead; 4 All of which when I heard, I was persuaded of one of these two, viz; either that you are God himself descended from heaven, who do these things, or the Son of God. 5 On this account therefore, I have written to you, earnestly to* desire you would take the trouble of a journey hither, and cure a disease which I am suffering from. 6 For I hear the Jews ridicule you, and intend you mischief. 7 My city is indeed small, but neat, and large enough for us both.

CHAPTER 2

The answer of Jesus by Ananais the footman to Abgarus the king, declining to visit the king.

Abgarus you are happy, forasmuch as you have believed in me, whom you have not seen. 2 For it is written concerning me, that those who have seen me should not believe in me, that they who have not seen might believe and live. 3 As to that part of your letter, which relates to my giving you a visit, I must inform you, that I must fulfil all the ends of my mission in this country, and after that be received up again to him who sent me. 4 But after my ascension I will send one of my disciples who will cure your disease, and give life to you, and all that are with you.

The Old Testament Trinity

Russian variant. Novgorod school. Egg tempera on beech. Burnished gold. 36 x 46 cm (1999)

THE MYSTICAL LANGUAGE OF ICONS

The icon called *The Hospitality of Abraham* or *The Old Testament Trinity*, is based on the incident referred to in Genesis 18: *"And the Lord appeared to him (Abraham) by the oaks of Mamre, as he sat at the door of his tent in the heat of the day. He lifted up his eyes and looked, and behold, three men stood in front of him. When he saw them, he ran from the tent door to meet them, and bowed himself to the earth, and said, 'My Lord, if I have found favour in your sight, do not pass by your servant'* (Gen 18, 1-3). Abraham took good care of his guests; he practised the virtue of hospitality (in Greek *philoxenia*) by receiving strangers in a friendly way. In the letter to the Hebrews this is commented thus: *'Do not neglect to show hospitality to strangers, for thereby some have entertained angels unawares'* (Heb 13, 2).

Sara was told that she should have a son, in spite of her old age. This promise achieved its final fulfilment in the annunciation to Mary.

According to Orthodox tradition, this event can be interpreted as a prefiguration of the Holy Trinity. The divine mystery which unfolds in the relationship between the three persons of the Godhead – Father, Son and Holy Spirit – was revealed to Abraham in the form of three visitors. In this way Abraham was given the privilege of seeing a living image of the Triune God. Man, who is created in the image of the Trinity, is thus a relational being, created with the ability to go beyond himself and love others.

John of Damascus points out the fundamental difference between God's being (essence) and his revealed form (energy) when he says: *'Abraham did not see the divine nature, for no man has ever seen God, but he saw an image of God and fell down and worshipped.'*

The icon depicts three winged and richly draped angels who sit at table. All turn towards three chalices which are placed in the middle, and they point towards these with their right hands. In their left hands they hold pastoral staffs. The central angel sits behind the table so that only the upper part of his body is visible, while the other two sit on thrones at either side. They rest their feet on a footstool. In addition to this central group of figures, we see a house, a tree and a mountain in the background. These elements are given forms which correspond to the figures in front of them. The figure to the left is characterised by a vertical posture like the house behind, while the other two bow their bodies lightly and repeat the curvature of the tree and the mountain. An invisible circle seems to enclose the three figures.

Other versions which emphasise the narrative aspect of the motif, include the servant who kills the calf and Abraham and Sara who serve the guests. Bodily positions, gestures and gazes express the continual and harmonious communication which exists between them. Wings, pastoral staffs and haloes indicate that Abraham's guests are heavenly beings. The angel to the left is traditionally identified as the Father – the source and final goal of all things. The central angel can be identified as the pre-existent Christ because of the cross in the halo and the conventional inscriptions IC XC. The circular composition enveloping them, symbolises divine attributes such as what is perfect, absolute, dynamic, self contained and infinite.

The depicted event transcends the natural limitations of time and space and contains several levels of meaning. The gathering around Abraham's table refers back to a sacred conversation which is thought to have taken place between the persons of the Trinity once in an unknown, eternal past. The Son points at the cup of suffering, bends towards the Father and thus expresses his willingness to be incarnated and restore mankind. The meal which Abraham prepared for his guests foreshadows the sacrament of the Eucharist, and the table is the altar where the sacrifice of Christ is commemorated. Furthermore the event can be seen as an anticipation of the heavenly meal in the world to come. Historically understood the building behind the angel to the left is Abraham's house (or tent). The allegorical meaning of the house can be the body of Mary which contained God, the appearance of God's Kingdom through the Church and the eternal dwellings Christ has in mind when he says: *'In my Father's house are many rooms'* (Jn 14, 2). Likewise the tree behind Christ can be the oak of Mamre, the tree of the holy cross or the tree of life in paradise. The mountain can be associated with decisive meetings between God and man both in the Old and the New Testaments (Sinai, Carmel and Tabor).

The Annunciation

Left:
Russian variant. Novgorod school.
Egg tempera on pine. Burnished gold.
78 x 110 cm (1993)

Right:
Detail of The Unborn Christ

*The Archangel
was sent to the pure Virgin
and with his greeting 'Hail'.
He brought good tidings,
that the Deliverer would come forth from her.
And so, accepting his salutation with faith,
she conceived Thee, the pre-eternal God,
who was pleased to become man
ineffably for the salvation of our souls.*

Aposticha from
The Small Vespers, tone 4.

The chief commander of the King's armies, the Archangel Gabriel, was sent to Mary to announce the Incarnation – God's coming to earth. According to Orthodox iconography Gabriel appeared to Mary when she was hand spinning with a spindle. The icon shows how she stops and listens to the angel's words: *'Do not be afraid Mary, for you have found favour with God. And behold, you will conceive in your womb and bear a son, and you shall call his name Jesus. He will be great, and will be called the Son of the Most High; and the Lord God will give to him the throne of his father David'* (Lk 1, 30-32).

The dialogue between Gabriel and Mary is the key to the mystery of the Incarnation. In the liturgy for this feast, Mary says: *'How shall my womb contain him whom the wide spaces of the heavens cannot contain?'* And the angel answers: *'O Virgin, let the tent of Abraham that once contained God teach you: for it prefigured your womb, which now receives the Godhead.'*

In the liturgical texts, Mary is addressed with several allegorical names which reflect her exalted role as *Theotokos – The Birthgiver of God*. She is called *"The Chariot and Dwelling of the Divinity, The Burning Bush that Remains Unconsumed, The Bridge that Leads to Heaven, The Ladder raised on high that Jacob saw, The Divine Jar of Manna, The Deliverance of the Curse and The Restorator of Adam."*

Mary's posture is humble and receptive. By saying yes to God's plan of salvation, she becomes a mediator between heaven and earth. The blue and red half-circle that directs rays of light towards her, symbolises God's supernatural intervention: *'The Holy Spirit will come upon you, and the power of the Most High will overshadow you; therefore the child to be born will be holy; the Son of God'* (Lk 1, 35).

The icon depicts how The King of Heaven has descended into Mary's womb and is seated there as a small Pantocrator on his throne.

The Archangel Gabriel

Russian variant. Novgorod school. Egg tempera on beech. 24 x 46 cm (1986)

Mother of God with resting Jesus

Serbian variant. Egg tempera on beech. 26.5 x 19 cm (1996)

Hail, enclosure of the God whom nothing can enclose:
Hail, gate of the hallowed mystery.
Hail, tidings doubted by unbelievers:
Hail, undoubted glory of the faithful.
Hail, most holy chariot of him who rides upon the cherubim:
Hail, best of all dwellings for him who is above the seraphim.
Hail, for thou bringest opposites to harmony:
Hail, for thou hast joined in one childbirth and virginity.
Hail, for through thee our sins is remitted:
Hail, for through thee Paradise is opened.
Hail, key of Christ's Kingdom:
Hail, hope of eternal blessings.
Hail, Bride without bridegroom!

From the Akathistos hymn to the Most Holy Theotokos

The Nativity of Christ

Model: mosaic from Chiesa della Martorana, Palermo
Egg tempera on beech. Burnished gold.
31 x 42 cm (1998)

This festival icon is based on the description of the birth of Jesus in Mark and Matthew, as well as on James' apocryphal gospel (ca 150 AD). According to James' gospel, Jesus was born in a mountain grotto. The icon depicts Mary half sitting, half lying on a pillow in the grotto. Mary who is noticeably bigger than the other figures is turned towards the swaddled child she holds. The child lies with his head against his mother's body. The high crib is shown in inverse perspective. An ox and a donkey are peering over the side of the crib. The rock formation is encircled by four angels with wings spread. To the left of the picture one angel is announcing the birth of Jesus to two of the shepherds. Farthest down on the left, at Mary's feet, sits Joseph resting his chin on his hand. His posture tells us that he is in deep thought. He is puzzling over the paradox of the Incarnation – that God permits himself to be born by a virgin. Farthest down on the right two women are bathing the child Jesus. The woman holding the child is testing the heat of the water. The wash bowl refers to the font and communion chalice and is also in inverse perspective. Even though Joseph and the women are placed in the foreground, they are only half the size of Mary.

The use of *hierarchical perspective* (the most important person having the central position and being exaggeratedly big) and *inverse perspective* (the diverging lines meeting in front of the picture, and not in a depth-creating vanishing point in the picture itself) are formal techniques to underline the theological content.

By descending down into matter, into creation, God allowed himself to be *'woven in the depths of the earth'* (Ps 139, 15). The expression *'depths of the earth'* refers here to the womb. Mary's womb is like a grotto in which God dwells. Mary is the Second Eve who brings God into the world, and by virtue of giving birth to God (*Theotokos*), Mary links man to the Creator in a new way. A liturgical text for the celebration of Christmas describes the response of the creation with the following words: *'What shall we offer you, Christ, who for our sake descended to earth as man? What creature of your creation thanks you? The angels offer you a hymn; the heavens a star, the wise men gifts, the shepherds their wonder; the earth, a grotto; the wilderness a crib: and we offer you a virgin mother.'*

God's unification with matter through the Incarnation is a turning point in the history of Salvation which includes all the created. The ox and the ass demonstrate that speechless animals can also recognize the Creator when he reveals himself: *'The ox knows its owner, and the donkey its master's crib; but Israel does not know, my people do not understand.'* (Is 1, 3).

The shepherds may be interpreted as representatives of the Jewish people, while the wise men from a foreign country who found the child Jesus by orientating themselves by a star, represent the heathens. The light beam that comes from the star at the top of the icon, strikes the child Jesus in the crib. Matthew describes how the star led the wise men who followed it, *'and there, ahead of them, went the star... until it stopped over the place where the child was'* (Mt 2, 9). The Apocryphal gospel of James tells us that Joseph went out to find a midwife. When they returned, the light in the grotto was so strong that *"their eyes could not bear it"* (Jas 14, 11). This blinding light is the same that overcame the apostles at the Transfiguration of Jesus.

The child Jesus in swaddling clothes might be associated with the dead body of Jesus which was swathed in linen, and the crib points forwards to the grave of Jesus. The close connection between Incarnation and Sacrifice becomes clear by looking at the crib as an image of the altar – the place for Christ's sacramental presence. Jesus is 'born' in the bread and wine each time the Eucharist is celebrated: *'I am the living bread that came down from heaven. Whoever eats of this bread will live forever; and the bread that I will give for the life of the world is my flesh'* (Jn 6, 51). Just as the hunger of the Jewish people was physically satisfied by the manna in the wilderness, so are the faithful spiritually satisfied by the body and blood of Jesus Christ at communion; *'the living bread which has come down from heaven'*.

Christ among the Doctors

Russian variant. Egg tempera on beech.
Burnished gold. 31 x 42 cm (1999)

*After three days
they found him in the temple,
sitting among the teachers,
listening to them
and asking them questions;
and all who heard him were amazed
at his understanding and his answers.*

Luke 2, 46-47

Christ of Silence

Russian variant. Egg tempera on beech.
27 x 35 cm (1999)

This uncommon iconographical type, *The Christ of Silence*, occurred in Russia during the 16th century. Other symbolic representations of Christ belonging to the same group are *Sophia, The Divine Wisdom* and *The Crucified Seraphim*.

Here the young, pre-existent Christ is depicted with wings, his hands crossed in front of his chest. The halo is inscribed with an eight-pointed star. The wings indicate that he resides in the angelic spheres while the eight-pointed star denotes his divinity. The crossed hands express a meditative and humble attitude which reflects the prophecy underlying this mystical motif: *'Behold my servant, whom I uphold, my chosen, in whom my soul delights; I have put my Spirit upon him, he will bring forth justice to the nations. He will not cry out or lift up his voice, or make it heard in the street'* (Is 42, 1-2). The icon communicates the profound willingness of Christ to submit to his passion in silence: *'He was oppressed, and he was afflicted, yet he opened not his mouth; like a lamb that is led to the slaughter, and like a sheep before its shearers is dumb, so he opened not his mouth'* (Is 53, 7).

The evangelist Luke, who describes several incidents from the childhood of Christ, tells how the twelve years old boy went with his parents to Jerusalem for the Feast of the Passover. Mary and Joseph did not notice that he lingered behind in Jerusalem as they returned to Nazareth.

The icon depicts the young boy sitting among the scholars in the temple discussing matters from the Scriptures. His central position, exaggerated size and didactic gesture reflect his importance and the impression he makes on those hearing him.

Christ acts here as the personification of *Sophia, The Divine Wisdom*. He reveals an extraordinary knowledge of the Scriptures and a spiritual insight witnessed only in those who have pondered the mysteries of God for a lifetime.

When his mother asks: *'Son, why have you treated us so?'* He answers surprisingly: *'How is it that you sought me? Did you not know that I must be in my Father's house?'* (Lk 2, 48-49). This reply discloses that Christ was conscious of his divine mission already at the age of twelve.

THE MYSTICAL LANGUAGE OF ICONS

Our Lady of the Sign

Left:
Greek. variant. Egg tempera on pine.
Burnished gold with punching.
45.5 x 61.5 cm (1996)

Right:
Cypriotic variant. Egg tempera on beech.
40.5 x 64 cm (1996)

*For he who before all time
radiated from the Father,
the only begotten Son,
it was he who was born
of you O Pure One,
and miraculously became flesh.
He who by nature is God,
also by nature became man
for our sake.*

Dogmaticon from
The Great Vigil, tone 6.

In this icon Mary is seen praying. On her breast is a circular medallion with an inset of the child Jesus. Mother and child are portrayed frontally. Their faces are compassionate and serious, marked by deep calmness and contemplation. It is not the intimacy between mother and child which is primary here, the focus of attention is Mary, who has been given the honourable title of *Theotokos* (The Birthgiver of God), and who is presenting the child to us as the Son of God. Another name for Mary is *Platytera* (Spacious, Wider than). The notion is that God, who could not be contained by the universe, found a place in Mary's body during her pregnancy. Thus no other human has been as close to God as Mary.

The title *Our Lady of the Sign* has its reference in a text from the prophet Isaiah 7, 14: *'The Lord himself will give you a sign. Behold a young woman shall conceive and bear a son, and shall call his name Immanuel.'* And as Christ came down to earth, God's promise that was mediated through Isaiah was fulfilled.

The initials above the shoulders of the child Jesus; IC – XC, are the first and last letters in the Greek spelling of Jesus Christ, and are a fixed attribute on all icons of Christ. Likewise the inscription above Mary; MHP – θY, is an abbreviation for the Mother of God. The stars on Mary's shoulders and her headdress symbolise her virginity before, during and after the birth and underline her unique position as the mother of a child with a divine origin.

This is the theological crux of the icon; with the mystery of the Incarnation, God voluntarily let himself be confined within time and space when becoming man through Jesus Christ. As a minor, he was already filled with divine insight. The icon does not primarily express the likeness of a portrait and thus associate the motif with a certain epoch and a certain place. The stylised facial expression, gesture and fall of the robes contributes to making the icon universal. The icon has its origin in an historic event, in this instance the Birth of Jesus, but the content is meant to have a universal relevance for all time. A quotation from St Augustine sums up the existential meaning thus: *'Of what help is it that Jesus was born, if he is not born within me?'*

Mother of God Hodegetria

Left:
Greek variant. Cretan school..
Egg tempera on oak. Burnished gold.
24 x 33 cm (1997)

Right:
Russian variant. Egg tempera on beech.
Burnished gold with punching.
27 x 35 cm (1999)

It is truly meet to bless you,
O Theotokos, ever blessed
and most pure,
and the Mother of our God.
More honourable
than the cherubim,
and more glorious beyond
compare than the seraphim:
without defilement
you gave birth to God the word:
true Theotokos we magnify you.

From the liturgy of John Crysostom

Among the many different versions in Orthodox iconography of Mary with the child Jesus, that of *The Mother of God Hodegetria* primarily underlines the formal relationship between mother and child. It is believed that the evangelist Luke painted the first version of this icon and that soon miraculous powers were ascribed to it after Mary had said: *'My blessing will always follow this icon.'* Perhaps this legend originated because Luke is the evangelist who gives most details about the childhood of Jesus. Probably his inside knowledge was acquired through direct contact with Mary.

The Mother of God supports the Son with her left arm while indicating him with her right hand. The Greek word *Hodegetria* meaning *she who shows the way,* refers to the raised position of the hand. The Son of God came to earth through *Theotokos* (The Birthgiver of God). Here she presents her Son to the world, while

they both gaze at each other lost in thought. The child Jesus sits upright supported by Mary's arm. He is clothed in a conventional, two-piece robe – a white tunic *(chiton)* with an orange outer garment *(himation)*. His right hand is raised in blessing, while he holds a scroll in his left one. These distinguishing characteristics signify that the child is both the pre-existent Logos (scroll) and the coming Saviour (the blessing sign).

The child's grown-up air makes visible the paradox of Christ's person; he is both God and man. The majesty of heaven is enthroned on Mary's arm. A text from the prophet Isaiah expresses this paradox with great clarity:
'For to us a child is born, to us a son is given; and the government will be upon his shoulder, and his name will be called Wonderful Counsellor, Mighty God, Everlasting Father, Prince of Peace' (Is 9, 6).

THE MYSTICAL LANGUAGE OF ICONS

Our Lady of Tenderness

Left:
Serbian variant.
Model: icon from
the iconostasis in
Decani monastery.
Egg tempera on beech.
Burnished gold.
27 x 35 cm (1999)

Right:
Greek variant.
Cretan school.
Model: icon by
Andreas Ritzos
or his circle.
Egg tempera on beech.
Burnished gold.
22 x 27 cm (1999)

The Greek word *eleousa* means *merciful,* while the equivalent Russian word *umilénie* may be translated with *mild, tender, loving, compassionate.* The emotional intensity of the icons presented here is a striking contrast to the more formalised renderings which mark types like *Our Lady of the Sign* and *Mother of God Hodegetria.*

Our Lady of Tenderness underlines the affectionate relationship between Mary and the child Jesus. Caressing postures and glances reveal their deep attachment to one another. The Saviour's identity as exalted Pantocrator takes second place. Instead we see that the Son of man is just as vulnerable and dependent on his mother as are all other children. He displays his need for intimacy and protection by nestling close to her. Both of them appear rather thoughtful while they rest together.

The psalm writer David compares his own soul with a contented child: *'But I have calmed and quieted my soul, like a child quieted at its mother's breast; like a child that is quieted is my soul'* (Ps 131, 2).

Children are normally playful, receptive and unprejudiced. Christ often refers to children and uses them as examples in his teaching. He obviously appreciates qualities like innocence, simplicity and trust. So he declares that *'unless you turn and become like children, you will never enter the kingdom of heaven. Whoever humbles himself like this child, he is the greatest in the kingdom of heaven'* (Mt 18, 5).

The Lord seems to identify himself spontaneously with a little boy when he takes him in his arms, saying: *'Whoever receives one such child in my name receives me'* (Mk 9, 37).

Mother of God
Pelagonitissa

From the region of Pelagonia
Also known as

Playful Infant

Serbian variant.
Egg tempera on beech.
Burnished gold.
30 x 40 cm (1999)

Left:

The Nursing
Mother of God

Greek variant.
Egg tempera on beech.
Burnished gold.
30 x 38 cm (2000)

The nursing Mother of God, in Greek *Galakto-trophusa,* literally means *She who nourishes with milk.* That is exactly what Mary is doing here – she uncovers her breast in order to nurse the child. By focusing on the close connection between mother and child, the true human nature of Christ is emphasised. Germanus of Constantinople stresses this same point when he writes that *'Christ did not just appear to be a man, like some kind of shadow, but he was really and truly a man.'* However, also the divine nature of Christ is suggested by his indeterminable age and the conventional gesture of blessing.

This rare motif can be associated with a text from the Gospel of Luke where we read that *'a woman in the crowd raised her voice and said to Jesus, "Blessed is the womb that bore you, and the breasts that you sucked!" But he said, "Blessed rather are those who hear the word of God and keep it!"'* (Lk 11, 27-28).

Mary kept the word of God in two ways. In addition to making her own body available for God, she also contemplated the divine mysteries *'in her heart'* – at the very centre of her personality. After the shepherds had told her what was said to them by the angels concerning the child, Luke writes: *'But Mary kept all these things, pondering them in her heart'* (Lk 2, 19).

The intimate relationship between Mary and the child Jesus can be seen as a metaphor of the Church and the devout. Hence the depiction of Mary nursing her baby becomes an expressive image of the Church feeding her spiritual children. The Church is a loving mother who gives birth to her children through baptism and nourishes them with the word of God and the Eucharist. In accordance with this metaphor the faithful are like sucklings who cannot survive or grow without the spiritual milk that their mother gives them.

Our Lady of Perpetual Help

Greek variant from Crete.
Egg tempera on oak. 34 x 47 cm
(1994)

The icon *Our Lady of Perpetual Help* originated on Crete in the last half of the 15th century. The motif gradually became widespread, also in the Western Catholic world. An early version is found above the high altar in the Redemptorist Church, San Alfonso in Rome. It takes its rudimentary form from *The Mother of God, Hodegetria*, but some new elements have been added which supplement the meaning of the content.

The child Jesus is resting, supported by Mary's left arm, but he holds no scroll, nor is his other hand raised in blessing, instead he is holding his mother's hand with both of his. His body is leaning forward, his ankles are crossed and one of his sandals has fallen off. His head is turned upwards to look at an angel displaying a cross. The archangel Gabriel, who earlier had explained the mystery of the Incarnation to Mary, explains the mystery of the cross to the future Saviour. The archangel Michael, directly opposite Gabriel, is holding a stalk of hyssop and a lance. This instrument of martyrdom

indicates the perfect sacrifice Christ will make in the future. The vision of torture and death gives rise to anxiety and the child Jesus seeks refuge with his mother. Anxiety about suffering and death is a deeply felt human reaction and may be interpreted as an expression of Christ's true human nature.

In the West this icon is also known as *Our Lady of the Passion*. Both titles say something about Mary's suffering and compassion. The pain she experiences at the thought of her son's future suffering, is pictured in the sorrowful expression on her face. It is as if she is already standing beneath the cross and living through the truth in Simeon's words: *'a sword will pierce your own soul too'* (Lk 2, 35).

Mary and the child Jesus refer to each other. The child demonstrates how The Mother of God gives security and protection to those who turn to her. With her humble answer to Gabriel, she is an example to all Christians: *'Here am I, the servant of the Lord; let it be with me according to your word'* (Lk 1, 38).

THE MYSTICAL LANGUAGE OF ICONS

Joseph with the Child Jesus

Melkite variant. Egg tempera on oak. 20 x 25 cm (1998)

This icon portrays the relationship between Joseph and the child Jesus. The way the child sits on his lap, brings to mind *The Mother of God Hodegetria* and *Our Lady of Perpetual Help*. The child seeks safety by placing both his hands in Joseph's right hand. Thus Joseph's special call is made apparent – that of providing protection and care for the Son of God who has allowed himself to be born as man.

The flowering lily is an attribute which may be connected with James' apocryphal gospel. The text describes how Joseph was chosen as Mary's bridegroom. All single men of David's line were invited to go to the temple with a dry stalk which they were to lay on the altar. The stalk which developed shoots and began to bloom, belonged to the one who was the chosen bridegroom. As confirmation that this sign was divinely inspired, the Lord himself descended from heaven as a dove: *'When he (Joseph) did bring his rod, and a dove coming from heaven pitched upon the top of it, every one plainly saw, that the virgin was to be betrothed to him.'* (Apocryphal James 6, 5).

Simeon with the Child Jesus

Russian variant. Egg tempera on oak (1989)

Simeon was in the temple when Mary and Joseph brought in the child Jesus to *'do for him what was customary under the law'*. St Luke tells us that the *'devout and righteous'* Simeon *'took the child in his arms and praised God.'* Thus Simeon was given the name *The Receiver of God.* He was the first to acknowledge that Jesus was the Messiah the Jews were awaiting. Simeon's song of praise expresses the fulfilment of the word of the prophet in a beautiful way: *'Master now you are dismissing your servant in peace, according to your word; for my eyes have seen*

your salvation, which you have prepared in the presence of all peoples, a light for revelation to the Gentiles and for the glory to your people Israel' (Lk 2, 29-30).

The melancholy expression on Simeon's face reflects his knowledge of Christ's future. He embraces the child and lays his cheek lovingly against its face. The old man has long hair and a beard and we see that his large head half fills the picture. In comparison, the child placed in the lower left corner appears very small, despite the conventional adult presentation.

The Fiery Ascent of the Prophet Elijah

Russian variant. Novgorod school.
Egg tempera on oak. 45.5 x 61.5 cm (1989)

THE MYSTICAL LANGUAGE OF ICONS

The Prophet Elijah

Greek variant. Cretan school.
Egg tempera on oak. 32.5 x 45 cm (1997)

The prophet Elijah emerges as an overshadowing giant among the prophets in the Old Testament. To punish the wickedness of King Ahab and Queen Jezebel, Elijah was given authority to stop the rain from falling. During the drought that followed he hid himself in the valley Cherith east of Jordan. Here, every morning and evening ravens brought Elijah bread and meat, and water he drank from a stream that ran through the valley. This icon portrays the prophet meditating on God's care. He sits at the entrance to a grotto in the wilderness, turned towards a bird which has become his servant. Elijah is distinguished by his ascetic way of life and close relationship with God. Both these features have been important sources of inspiration for hermits and different monastic orders throughout time. In hagiographic literature there are many examples of wild animals having co-existed peacefully with holy ascetics. Such examples reflect the harmony found between man and the rest of creation before the fall, at the same time as it points towards a new order that will characterise life in the world to come.

When Elijah met the Baal priests in spiritual combat on Mount Carmel, he challenged them by saying that *'the God who answers by fire is indeed God'* (1 Kings 18, 24). In answer to the prophet's fervent prayers, fire came down from heaven.

The icon on the left depicts how Elijah was taken up alive to heaven in a chariot of fire, while his disciple Elisha watched: *'As they continued walking and talking, a chariot of fire and horses of fire separated the two of them, and Elijah ascended in a whirlwind into heaven'* (2 Kings 2, 11). This event may be understood as a prefigration of Christ's ascension. The prophet's sojourn in the desert, the miracle of the meal and oil at Zarephath, and the restoring to life of a dead boy have clear parallels in the life of Jesus.

Fire is a cleansing and transforming power which is often seen in connection with God's being: *'Now the appearance of the glory of the Lord was like a devouring fire on the top of the mountain in the sight of the people of Israel'* (Ex 24, 17). The fire on Mount Carmel and the chariot of fire that took Elijah up to heaven are expressions of God's uncreated energy (*dynamis*). This energy may be understood as a divine form of revelation (*theophany*). St John of Damascus compares the saints with red-hot iron. Iron that is made red-hot by fire is still iron, but unlike iron that has become cold, it can be moulded. The saints do not lose their identities as individuals by striving to become one with God.

The pre-existent Christ is portrayed in a blue semicircle at the very top of the icon. His arms are outstretched in blessing and it appears that he is drawing Elijah up to him with the aid of all the beams coming out of the heavenly sphere. The winged horses drawing the chariot are just as glowing as the flames surrounding the prophet. To the left we see how Elisha, who had prayed for a double portion of the Master's spirit, clutches his cape tightly as he disappears. Thus was the power of the predecessor transferred to the heir in a highly concrete manner. When Elisha later struck the river Jordan with his cape, the waters parted to allow him to cross dry-footed. The river is depicted as a blue, rectangular area in the green countryside. A raven, with a bread in its mouth, is depicted on the far right.

John the Baptist in the Wilderness

Greek variant. Egg tempera on wood. 30 x 42 cm

THE MYSTICAL LANGUAGE OF ICONS

John the Baptist

Greek variant.
Egg tempera on oak. 27 x 37 cm

From before he was born, John the Baptist had been chosen to prepare the Israelites for the coming of the Messiah. In their old age, his parents, Zachariah and Elizabeth, were told by the angel Gabriel that they would have a son *'With the spirit and power of Elijah'* (Lk 1, 17). John the Baptist's deeds as a prophet indicates the transition from the Old to the New Covenant. His austere way of life, as well as his chastising manner of teaching are reminiscent of the prophet Elijah.

Elizabeth and Mary, the Mother of Jesus, were close relatives. In connection with a meeting that took place between these two women while they were pregnant (The Visitation) it is said that on hearing Mary's greeting Elizabeth cried out, and: *'the child leapt in her womb.'* (Lk 1, 44). Even before he was born John reacted to the coming Saviour whom he would later point to saying *'Behold, the Lamb of God who takes away the sin of the world!'* (Jn 1, 29)

The baptism of Jesus in the river Jordan marks the pinnacle of John the Baptist's life. In Greek tradition he has been given the title *Prodromos* meaning *Forerunner*, or directly translated *in advance*. He was also called the Angel of the Wilderness, which means the Messenger from the Wilderness. The Greek word *angelos* may be translated with *angel* or *messenger*. The wings John has in this icon are to underscore his role as messenger.

John the Baptist lived as an ascetic in the wilderness, clothed himself in camel hair and ate locusts and wild honey. In this icon he is portrayed according to convention, and has a thin face, an intense gaze and long shaggy hair and beard. Paradoxically he holds his own head on a tray. Because he dared to reprimand King Herod for breaking his marriage vows, he was thrown into prison and later beheaded. This apparently inconsistent presentation shows that an icon treats not only space, but also time as relative. John is depicted here in three different time dimensions simultaneously. The icon records his earthly life, his martyrdom and following sojourn in the realm of the dead and also his present status as a saint in heaven.

John urged the people to repent (in Greek *metanoia*) and baptised those who confessed their sins. The essence of his teaching is written on the scroll in his hand: *'Repent, for the kingdom of heaven has come near'* (Mt 3, 2).

The Baptism of Christ

Greek variant. Cretan school.
Egg tempera on pine.
78.5 x 120 cm (1989)

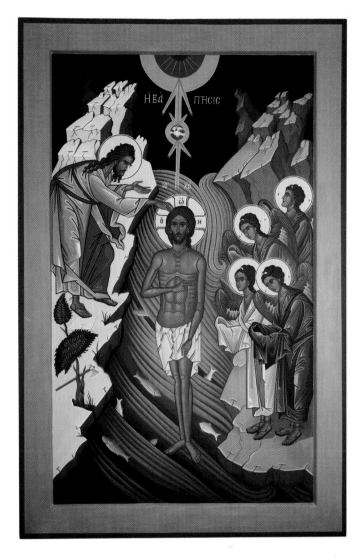

The river Jordan once turned back
before the mantle of Elisha,
after Elijah had been taken up
into heaven
and the waters were divided
on this side and on that:
the stream became a dry path before him,
forming a true figure of the baptism
whereby we pass over
the changeful course of life.
Christ has appeared in the Jordan
to sanctify the waters.

From the Liturgy for the Baptism of Christ

The feast for the Baptism of Jesus is celebrated on 6 January and is one of the great feasts of the Church year. As well as marking the transition to the public life of Jesus, the occasion is regarded as an *epiphany* (Greek for revelation) or *theophany* (the revelation of God or his appearance) It is the divine identity of Christ and the dynamism between the persons in the Trinity which manifest themselves here. The dogma that refers to the Trinity was formulated at the Council in Constantinople in 381 AD.

The invisible Father points to the Son by letting his voice be heard, saying: *'This is my Son, the Beloved, with whom I am well pleased'* (Mt 3, 17). The Holy Spirit is represented symbolically by a dove hovering over the Son.

In accordance with iconographic convention, the river Jordan is framed by rocky countryside on both sides. The diagonally flowing water surrounds Jesus, but characteristically enough it does not cover his body. From the half-circle at the very top of the icon a powerful beam of light shines down. It is broken by a medallion with an inset dove. This central axis is continued in the noble figure of Christ, who is presented frontally. In this way we see how the Holy Spirit unites the Father with the Son.

John the Baptist stands on the left bank, bending humbly forward to lay his hands on Christ's head, while four angels on the rocky bank opposite cover their hands as a sign of adoration and reverence.

By walking down into the river Jordan, down into matter, Christ makes known the depth of his identification with man and creation. He allows himself to be covered in the water and thus fills it with his divine presence. Heaven is united with the earth. He blesses the water and gives it a sacramental dimension, just as he later blesses the bread and wine.

The Transfiguration

Russian variant. Novgorod school.
Egg tempera on oak. 50 x 70 cm (1989)
Aylesford Priory, England

Transfigured thou hast made Adam's nature,
which was grown dim,
to shine once more as lightning,
transforming it into the
glory and splendour of thy Godhead.

From The Liturgy for The Transfiguration

The Synoptics tell us that Jesus took the three apostles Peter, James and John, those he was closest to, and led them up a high mountain. There he was transfigured into blinding light; both his face and clothing changing before their eyes.

Matthew writes that *'his face shone like the sun, and his clothes became dazzling white'* (Mt 17, 2). Mark comments that his clothes were *'such as no one on earth could bleach them'* (Mk 9, 3). And Luke describes how the Transfiguration took place while praying: *'And while he was praying, the appearance of his face changed, and his clothes became dazzling white'* (Lk 9, 29).

Then there before the eyes of the apostles appeared the Old Testament prophets Moses and Elijah talking to Jesus. However, only Luke mentions that they talked about the fate awaiting Jesus in Jerusalem, and that the apostles fell into a deep sleep when they saw them. But all of them tell us that Peter in his fear and confusion suggested building a dwelling for each of the three men who appeared before them.

However, the disciples were to become even more afraid when a bright cloud threw its shadow over them, and they heard a voice speaking to them from the cloud: *'This is my Son, the Beloved; with him I am well pleased; listen to him!'* (Mt 17, 5). Matthew is the evangelist who describes most clearly how the apostles reacted when he writes that *'When the disciples heard this, they fell to the ground and were overcome by fear'* (Mt 17, 6). When the vision is over and Jesus again is alone with the apostles, he comforts them saying: *'Get up and do not be afraid'* (Mt 17, 7).

The composition for this icon follows a strictly symmetrical scheme. A stylised mountainous landscape characterised by several stair-like landings forms the background for the incident. Christ stands – or almost floats – on the central peak. He is clothed in a dazzling white robe and surrounded by a mandorla in different shades of blue. On his left he is flanked by Elijah, and on his right by Moses, each standing on his own mountain peak. Three beams of light radiate from the mandorla, each one striking one of the disciples. On the far left, we see James lying on his back after his fall. He covers his face with his hands to prevent him seeing more. John who fell head over heels, supports himself with his right hand and covers his face with the other, while Peter rises up from a kneeling position and raises his right hand to speak.

The Latin word *transfiguratio* can be translated by 'to be changed into another form', while the Greek word *metamorphosis* means 'to progress from one state of being to another'. The Transfiguration is a revelation of Christ's divine nature, a manifestation of the Trinity, and confirmation of the continuity between the Old and the New Testaments.

Christ lets his disciples catch a glimpse of a supernatural light with transforming power – they were not blinded by natural sunlight, but by the uncreated light that has its source in God's own being. Because of his divine identity, Christ is himself that light: *'For in him the whole fullness of the Godhead dwells bodily'* (Col 2, 9).

The disciples heard the Father, saw the Son and were enveloped by the Holy Spirit in the brilliant sky. They also witnessed Moses and Elijah, who represent The Law and The Prophets, confirm that Christ fulfilled the Messianic promises. Because of the Incarnation, the God they had served so faithfully without seeing could now be seen and spoken to, face to face.

Moses and Elijah had experienced how God had revealed himself indirectly through supernatural light phenomena in the Old Covenant. The burning bush, the pillar of fire that led Israel through the wilderness, the light Moses saw on Mount Sinai, the fire on Mount Carmel and the chariot of fire that lifted Elijah up to heaven are examples of such uncreated energies. In the blinding light on Mount Tabor the prophets could contemplate God's personified radiance directly.

THE MYSTICAL LANGUAGE OF ICONS

The Raising of Lazarus

Russian variant. Novgorod school. Egg tempera on beech. Burnished gold. 36 x 46 cm (1999)

THE MYSTICAL LANGUAGE OF ICONS

According to the Gospel of John (Jn 11), *The Raising of Lazarus* took place in the small town of Bethany near Jerusalem. Lazarus and his sisters Mary and Martha were among Christ's closest friends, and they often received him in their home. The city wall can be glimpsed between the two rocks that make up the scenery for the event. Christ, wearing his conventional red tunic and blue cloak, enters from the left followed by his disciples. First among them we see Peter; he can be recognised by his yellow garment. Christ lifts his right arm in a commanding gesture and directs his eyes at Lazarus who comes forth from the tomb. Mary and Martha have fallen down at the feet of the Master. A young man lifts the stone away from the tomb while another seizes the edge of the grave clothes and covers his mouth with his cloak as if to hold back his reaction – or perhaps in order to dull the stench of the corpse. Behind him there is a group of Jews who had come to comfort the sisters in their grief. Now they witness how the Lord of life triumphs over death. The impression this made on them can be seen in their gestures. Some lift their arms in wonder, some stare at Christ, while others look with fright at the dead man returning to life.

The Jews were not unfamiliar with signs and mighty works in their religious tradition, yet a miracle like this was unprecedented: *'Who has ever known or heard of a man raised from the dead, when his corpse already stank? Elijah and Elisha raised the dead, yet not from the tomb or four days after death'* (Great Compline, canticle 4).

The icon reproduced here depicts with great detail the very moment when Christ cries with a loud voice, *'Lazarus, come out!'* (Jn 11, 43). On this occasion Christ does not conceal his supernatural capability, as when he raised the daughter of Jairus, but he demonstrates it publicly. By thus establishing a reason for hope, he gives the disciples and the others who believe a key to understanding the meaning of his passion on the cross.

This powerful sign provoked two completely different reactions among those who witnessed it: namely faith and denunciation: *'Many of the Jews therefore, who had come with Mary, and had seen what he did, believed in him; but some of them went to the Pharisees and told what*

Jesus had done... So from that day on they took counsel how to put him to death (Jn 11, 45-46, 53).

Of all the miracles Christ performed, *The Raising of Lazarus* is the only one which is incorporated into the range of the twelve liturgical feasts. Hence the profoundly symbolic significance attributed to it by the Church is reflected.

The Raising of Lazarus is celebrated on the Saturday before Palm Sunday and foreshadows the dramatic events of Easter week where the theme is the death and resurrection of Christ himself. Both *The Raising of Lazarus* and *The Descent into Hell* demonstrates the triumph of Christ over death. This thematic parallel is emphasized in the liturgical texts: *'The palaces of hell were shaken, when in its depths Lazarus began once more to breathe, straightaway restored to life by the sound of Thy voice.'* (Great Compline, canticle 2).

The Raising of Lazarus also has an obvious escatological dimension in that it anticipates the general resurrection on the last day. Mary has this hopeful perspective in mind when she in her dialogue with Christ confirms that she believes in the resurrection of the dead.

Furthermore, the liturgical texts proclaim how the two natures of Christ can be deduced from this particular story. By shedding tears he displays true human emotions. John simply writes that *'Jesus wept'* (Jn 11, 35). The people standing by clearly see his grief and agitation and exclaim: *'See how he loved him!'* (Jn 11, 36). His humanity is not only an outer appearance, but part of his essential identity. Simultaneously he manifests his divine nature by calling Lazarus forth from the grave. Although Christ has foreknowledge of his friend's death, he pretends as if ignorant and asked where they have laid him: *'As man, Thou hast shed tears for Lazarus; as God, Thou hast raised him up. Thou hast asked, "Where is he buried, dead these four days?" thus confirming our faith in Thine Incarnation'* (Great Compline, canticle 4).

The Maker of man, who in the beginning *'joined dust to spirit and breathed into the clay a living soul'* by his word, performs a divine act that refers back to the creation of man when he raises Lazarus from the dead. (Great Compline, canticle 5).

Long before it actually happened, the prophet Zechariah foresaw the paradoxical character of *The Entry of Christ into Jerusalem: 'Rejoice greatly, O daughter of Zion! Shout aloud, O daughter of Jerusalem! Lo, your king comes to you; triumphant and victorious is he, humble and riding on an ass, on a colt the foal of an ass'* (Zech 9, 9). A king who is riding on a donkey, an ordinary working animal, sounds like a contradiction. Nevertheless, before Pilate Christ himself proclaims that: *'My kingship is not of this world'* (Jn 18, 36). This point is also stressed in the liturgy for Palm Sunday: *'He who sits upon the throne of the cherubim, for our sake sits upon a foal; and coming to his voluntary Passion, today he hears the children cry "Hosanna!" while the crowd replies, "O Son of David, make haste to save those whom Thou hast created"'* (Mattins, tone 8).

There is little in the festivity of Palm Sunday resembling the imperial custom of riding into the city after a great military victory. The proud commander would allow himself to be cheered by the people, and triumphant soldiers bearing weapons would be followed by prisoners and spoils of war. Compared with such a display of power, the contrast to *The Entry into Jerusalem* is striking. Christ does not surround himself with armed guards or impressive symbols of authority, but is attended by disciples who barely understand the intentions of their own Master. Such insight came later, after his ascension to heaven. *'Jesus of Nazareth, the King of the Jews'* (Jn 19, 19), is humble and compassionate. Knowing beforehand the fate of Jerusalem, he weeps over it. The people who rejoice when they see him are not obedient subjects, but an unstable crowd who a few days later will turn against him.

In this icon Christ comes riding from the right. He sits on the back of the donkey like a king on his throne. The two-piece robe, the scroll and the gesture of blessing are well known attributes in the iconography of the Pantocrator. His body is depicted frontally; only the direction of the gaze and a slight turn of the head disclose that he is on his way to the city before him. He is flanked by Peter and John, who in this case represent all the disciples.

The scenery is simple – almost minimalistic. Apart from the wavy field of grass, this icon has no actual landscape. Most versions of this particular motif show the riding Christ and his disciples in front of a mountain. Here they appear to float above the earth, clearly standing out from the gilded background. A striking feature is that neither the donkey nor the disciples touch the ground with their feet. However, the crowd welcoming, does so. A group of six adults and four children represent the multitude of people. Many of them are holding palm branches in their hands – an ancient symbol of victory. Between the two groups there is a single palm tree into which a child has climbed. In front of the company a young boy comes running, spreading a garment on the ground. Within Byzantine iconography this symbolic act, which is meant to demonstrate the appointment of a king (2 Kings 9, 13), is only performed by children. This convention corresponds with the teaching of Christ when he says that *'whoever does not receive the kingdom of God like a child shall not enter it'* (Mk 10, 15).

Jerusalem is depicted as a cylindrically shaped fortress rising behind the group to the left. The city gate is open. A few houses, a couple of towers and a cupola constitute Jerusalem as a whole. The half circle with bowmen's crenelles on it overarching the city is the furthermost city wall. Consequently Jerusalem is seen both frontally and from above. This inconsistent perspective, as well as the other features, indicate that Jerusalem is represented mainly as a symbol.

According to the spiritual writer John Cassian (c. 365–435) *The Entry into Jerusalem* may be interpreted on four different levels. The first, *literal* level refers to the historic event, namely that of Christ who rode in procession into the Jewish capital Jerusalem and was acclaimed as king by the crowd a few days before his crucifixion. On the *allegorical* or *typological* level Jerusalem stands for the Church that Christ established by his death and resurrection, and with which he unites himself through word and sacraments during every divine service. On the *moral* or *tropological* level, Jerusalem is the individual human soul that receives Christ in a spiritual way. On the last, *analogical* level Jerusalem refers to the eternal abodes in the world to come – the heavenly Jerusalem where the Kingdom of God will blossom in its fullness.

The Entry into Jerusalem

Greek variant. *Model:* mosaic from the Monastery of Dafni, Athens. Egg tempera on beech. 36 x 46 cm. (1999)

Processional Cross

Egg tempera on wood.
44 x 58 cm (1990)

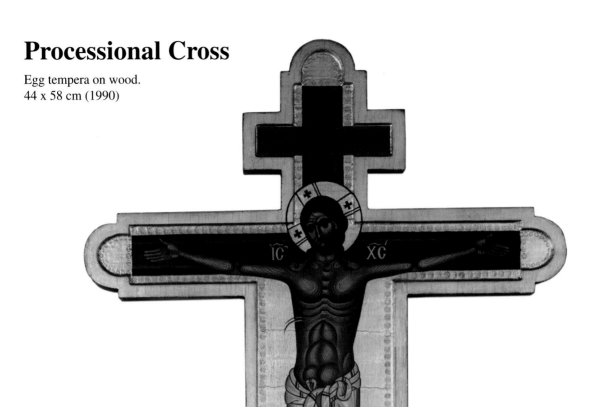

On this procession crucifix, Christ demonstrates that he is the victor of death. He does not hang from the cross, he stands and shows no signs of suffering. His eyes are open, his arms stretched straight out and his feet are parallel. His head inclines slightly to one side and his posture may be interpreted as a welcoming, inviting gesture. Such an interpretation reflects Jesus' own words from the Gospel of John: *'And I, when I am lifted up from the earth, will draw all men to myself'* (Jn 12, 32).

The inscription (in Hebraic, Latin and Greek) which Pilate allowed to be fastened to the cross is reproduced in Latin: *Iesus Nazarenus Rex Iudeorum* – Jesus of Nazareth, King of the Jews. The title of king indicates triumph, but Christ's triumph is a paradox and a mystery, because it was won through suffering and death. The martyrs demonstrate this paradox when they gain life by losing it.

John who was an eye witness to the drama on Calvary tells us that the wound in Christ's side was inflicted after his death (Jn 19, 33-37). Therefore, strictly speaking, it is historically incorrect to depict the crucified Christ with open eyes and a bleeding wound. However, by ignoring sequential time, the deeper meaning becomes even more apparent. The cross is like an altar where the sacrifice was made, and Christ himself is both the sacrifice and the priest who brings the offering. When the crucified Christ is portrayed as awake and with an open wound in his side, it is a manifestation of Christ's living presence in the Eucharist. It is the resurrected and living Christ who gives himself in the bread and the wine.

Just as God opened Adam's side and formed Eve, so has the Church, also called the second Eve and Christ's bride, has its origin in Christ's open wound. Through the act of offering himself on the cross, Christ demonstrates the very essence of love. And the Church is called upon to pass on that divine love for *'Love never ends'* (1 Cor 13, 8).

Epitaphios

Model: embroidered
Serbian epitaphios (lament
over the dead Christ).
Egg tempera on oak.
28 x 44 cm (1989).

The dead Christ is surrounded by grieving cherubim and angels singing the Trisagion: Holy, holy, holy! In Orthodox liturgy, a beautifully decorated coffin with a motif of the dead Christ is placed in the Church on Good Friday. Usually this motif is an embroidered cloth. This concrete liturgical re-enacting of the Easter drama allows the faithful to feel some of the sorrow experienced by Mary, John and Joseph of Arimathea.

'Joseph with Nicodemus
took Thee down from the Tree,
who deckest Thyself with light
as with a garment,
and looking upon Thee dead, stripped,
and without burial,
in his grief and tender compassion
he lamented.'

From the Good Friday Vesper

ὉΕΠΙΤΆΦΙΟϹ   ΘΡΙΝΟϹ

Lamentation at the Grave of Christ

Model: icon of Emmanuel Lambardos, Cretan School (16 c). Egg tempera on beech. 40 x 49 cm (1986)

The icon with the title *Epitaphios* or *Lamentation at the Grave of Christ* is a convincing and deeply moving presentation of how Mary, John and the others who were close to Christ may have expressed their grief after he was taken down from the cross. The origin of this motif is found in a picture sequence describing Mary's life. The evangelists do not dwell on the details surrounding the burial of Christ. They say nothing about the Mother of Jesus or the other women who were present and grieved, but they mention that Joseph of Arimathea asked Pilate for permission to remove the body from the cross. John writes that Nicodemus was also there, and that he had with him a mixture of myrrh and aloes with which to anoint the body (Jn 19, 39). Mark writes that *'Mary Magdalene and Mary the Mother of Joset saw where the body was laid'* (Mk 15, 47).

In the icon painting handbook *Hermeneia*, Dionysios of Fourna (active in the 17th century) explains how the motif is to be executed. The icon shown above, conforms closely to the instructions in this text: *'A large, rectangular stone with a cloth spread out on it. On this Christ lies on his back, his upper body naked, and the All Holy (Mary) on her knees bends over him and kisses his face. Joseph (of Arimathea) kisses his feet and John the Theologian kisses his right hand. Behind Joseph, Nicodemus leans on a ladder gazing at Christ. Next to the All Holy, Mary Magdalene throws up her hands and weeps, while the other women carrying herbs tear at their hair. Behind them is the cross with the inscription. Below Christ lies Nicodemus' basket with the nails, pliers and hammer in it. Beside it is another wooden vessel that is rather like a small wine goblet.'*

The King of Glory

Greek variant.
Egg tempera on oak. 17.5 x 23.5 cm (1994)

The dead Christ has recently been taken down from the cross. The head lies on one shoulder, the eyes are shut and the arms are crossed over the chest. The open wounds in the hands and side express Christ's *kenosis*, that he has emptied his body by submitting to death. The redeeming quality of the water and the blood that ran out of the wound in his side, is passed on by the sacraments of Baptism and the Eucharist. The hysop stalk and the lance, the arm of the cross and the nails make Christ's suffering visible. The inscription above the halo is an abbreviation of *The King of Glory*. This motif, also called *The Most Humble* or *The Man of Pain*, is usually placed in a niche behind the altar where the priest prepares the Eucharist. The icon invites meditation on Christ's sacrifice and his victory over death.

Let the same mind be in you
that was in Christ Jesus,
who though he was in the form
of God, did not regard equality
with God as something to be
exploited, but emptied himself,
taking the form of a slave,
being born in human likeness.

And being found in human form,
he humbled himself
and became obedient
to the point of death –
even death on the cross.

Therefore God also highly
exalted him
and gave him the name
that is above every name,
so that at the name of Jesus
every knee should bend,
in heaven and on earth
and under the earth,
and every tongue should confess
that Jesus Christ is Lord,
to the glory of God the Father.

Phil 2, 5-11

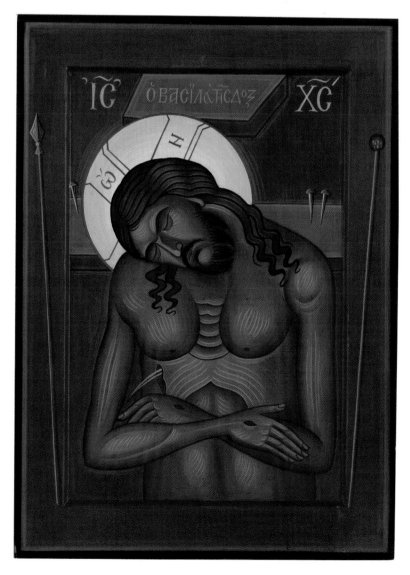

The De

Triptych icon. Egg tempera on wood. 80 x 40

This triptych formed icon is a simplified version of a complicated motif which usually has a large gallery of figures. It shows a white-clad Christ as he descends to the Realm of the Dead to free the first human couple from the prison of death. He is surrounded by a glowing mandorla. The mandorla and his white robes symbolise the Saviour's state of glory. He stamps triumphantly on the gates over the abyss of Hell which lie broken, grasps Adam and Eve's wrists and raises them up. Keys, nails, chains and hindrances lie spread about everywhere. The central panel is flanked by two doors; Abel is portrayed on the right-hand one and John the Baptist on the left-hand one. Each stands – or floats – above his own sarcophagus. Abel may be interpreted as a prefiguration of Christ's sacrifice on the cross. The shepherd Abel sacrificed a lamb from his flock for God and was himself an offering when his jealous brother Cain killed him. The first man to experience the reality of death, meets here the victor of death. John the Baptist, who points towards Christ in his earthly life, does so also in the realm of death.

to Hell

o from Kariye Djami in Constantinople (1996)

The apostle Peter wrote that Christ *'went and made a proclamation to the spirits in prison'*. Peter reminds us that the work of redemption includes all people, *for 'the gospel was proclaimed even to the dead'* (1 Pt 3, 19 and 4, 6). Apart from these short Bible texts, the iconography builds mainly upon the apocryphal gospel according to Nicodemus, in which Christ's triumph over Satan and the Kingdom of Death is described as a grand drama.

The Incarnation, God's visible appearance as a man, was a form of divine descent consisting of many steps. When Christ let himself be baptised, he subjected himself to the condition of sinful man. And further, by going down into the water, he let himself be covered in matter. He took still one more step down when he was buried in the depths of the earth. But by descending into Hell, Christ reached, existentially, life's deepest abyss. From the abysmal depths he arose from the grave and later attained life's highest peak when he ascended to heaven and took his seat on the throne of heaven.

THE MYSTICAL LANGUAGE OF ICONS 73

The Doubting of Thomas

Russian variant. Novgorod school. Egg tempera on beech. Burnished gold. 36 x 46 cm. (1999)

After his resurrection, Christ on different occasions showed himself to his anxious disciples, thereby assuring them of his continual presence. They were reluctant to believe, however, and Thomas openly demanded a proof.

In the icon reproduced here, we see how Thomas is cured of his incredulity. The cloak hanging over the wall and roof top denotes that the event takes place indoors, and the trees behind the wall indicate the same. This significant point is clearly shown in the design of this icon. Christ stands on a footstool in front of a shut door. Sometimes this motif is actually called *The Shut Door*. The disciples had locked themselves up for fear of the Jews, nevertheless the risen body of Christ was capable of penetrating matter. In spite of this supernatural feature, Christ several times, when encountering his disciples, insisted that he was not a spirit, but a real person with a physical body. He demonstrated this by eating something they had prepared, like fish or a honey cake. Although he was able to enter through shut doors, his body still carried the scars of the crucifixion. Hence he was recognisable.

When Peter, John and the others declared that they had seen the resurrected one, Thomas refused to believe. He had not been present. For him it was not enough to hear the testimony of his fellow disciples in order to believe; not even to see the risen Christ with his own eyes would necessarily convince him. He went a step further and stated that unless I *place my finger in the mark of the nails, and place my hand in his side, I will not believe'* (Jn 20, 25).

When after eight days Christ all of a sudden appeared again among the stunned disciples, Thomas was with them. Christ did not rebuke Thomas for his lack of faith, but instead invited him to confirm the reality of his presence by touching the wounds: *'Put your finger here, and see my hands; and put out your hand, and place it in my side; do not be faithless, but believing.'* Thomas answered him, *'My Lord and my God!'* (Jn 20, 27-28).

The icon depicts the moment when the risen Christ uncovers his side so that Thomas can see and touch the wound left by the spear. The title of this icon – *The Doubting of Thomas* – is also referred to as *The Convincing of Thomas,* thus marking his transition from disbelief to belief. The other disciples stand on either side, witness-

ing how the Master, with this moving gesture, manifests both his divine and his human nature.

Thomas challenges the Lord, and Christ generously displays his tortured and glorified body. However, after the ascension, there is no longer direct access to his physical presence. Those seeking the risen Christ will have to rely on the word of those who witnessed it. Christ has those in mind who at a later stage will come to believe in him when he says: *'Have you believed because you have seen me? Blessed are those who have not seen and yet believe'* (Jn 20, 29).

Modern man can easily identify himself with the doubt and hesitation of Thomas. His struggle makes him a comforting figure. He does not accept what he is told straightaway, but wants to investigate for himself. Thus eagerly seeking the truth, in the end he finds it.

Gregory the Great (c. 540-604) comments on this particular aspect in a homily: *'The considerable time it took for the disciples to believe in the Lord's Resurrection may have been a weakness on their part; nevertheless, it served to our strength. In response to their doubts, they received numerous proofs of the Resurrection: when we become aware of them, we can say that the apostles' doubts are the opportunity for us to affirm out faith. Mary Magdalen, who believed immediately, is less useful to us than Thomas, who doubted for some time. For this doubt led him to touch Christ's wounds, thereby healing in our hearts the wound of doubt'* (Homily 29).

St George and the Dragon

Egg tempera on beech. Novgorod school.
31 x 42 cm (1998)

St George came from Cappodocia in present day Turkey, where he served as an officer under the Emperor Diocletian and was honoured for his courage and ability. But when he persuaded the Empress Alexandra to convert to Christianity, the Emperor instigated a brutal persecution which ended in the martyrdom of both George and Alexandra, probably in Lydda in Palestine in the year 303. Under torture George was brave and enduring, and in the Eastern Church this popular saint was given the title of Great Martyr.

Often when George is presented as a knight on a white horse, it is as an apocalyptic imitation of Christ (Rev 19, 11). The dragon is an image of personified evil; *'that ancient serpent, who is the Devil and Satan'* (Rev 20, 2).

According to legend George was supposed to have killed a dragon that terrorised a village by demanding human sacrifices. In a more embroidered version of this motif, a princess is to be the dragon's next victim. But the fearless George intervenes, kills the dragon and saves the princess. After this deed the whole village elected to be baptised.

George has the status of patron saint for knights and soldiers, but as the name is derived from a Greek word meaning farmer, farmers have also regarded George as their patron saint. St George has his feast day on 23rd April.

THE MYSTICAL LANGUAGE OF ICONS

Daniel in the Lion's Den

Egg tempera on beech.
Novgorod school. 31 x 75 cm (1998)

During the exile of the Jews in Babylon (500 BC), Daniel had a central position as advisor to the King's Court *'because he was faithful, and no negligence or corruption could be found in him'* (Dan 6, 4). Envious officials who wanted him displaced could find no cause for complaint. However, they knew that Daniel was a God-fearing man and they had the king sign an order that whosoever prayed to any other than the king would be cast into the lion's den. Trapped by his own words and against his will, the king felt obliged to cast Daniel into the lion's den.

This motif is conspicuous for its use of hierarchical perspective. Daniel is portrayed so big that there is not even room for him in the den. The lions have met their master and instead of attacking they lick his feet and thus demonstrate that they submit to one who, in the spiritual sense, is bigger and stronger than they are.

From a typological reading of the text, the description of Daniel in the lion's den is a prefiguration of Christ's descent into Hell. The innocent Daniel returns unharmed from the evil treatment he was exposed to. The story of Joseph in the well and the prophet Jonah in the belly of the fish may be interpreted in the same way. They were both cast down into a life-threatening abyss, but God came to their aid, and they themselves were the cause of saving others. Daniel, Joseph and Jonah are examples of Old Testament saviour types, precursors of the victorious Christ.

THE MYSTICAL LANGUAGE OF ICONS

The Archangel Michael

Greek variant.
Egg tempera on oak. 27 x 35 cm (1998)

The Archangel Gabriel

Greek variant.
Egg tempera on oak. 27 x 35 cm (1989)

The Archangel Michael has the prestige of being head of the angels, God's attending spirits. The word archangel comes from the Greek word *arché* (prince) and *angelos* (messenger). The Hebraic meaning of the name Michael is *'Who is like God'*. The prophet Daniel wrote *'Michael, the great prince'* who shall arise at the time of the end (Dan 12, 1). This angel is a very giant who is always bidden to fight against God's enemies; Satan, the demons and *'the spiritual forces of evil in the heavenly places'* (Eph 6, 12). In the letter of Jude it is told that *'the archangel Michael contended with the devil and disputed about the body of Moses'* (Jude 9). St John describes how *'Michael and his angels fought against the dragon... The great dragon was thrown down, that ancient serpent, who is called the Devil and Satan, the deceiver of the whole world'* (Rev 12, 7-9).

On the icon on the left he wears richly decorated armour, his sword is at the ready and intense concentration radiates from the face. His whole being is focused on carrying out God's will.

Whereas Michael was sent out to fight against God's enemies, Gabriel was sent with good tidings to God's chosen. In Hebrew the name Gabriel means 'God's power'.

The archangel Gabriel went to Zechariah and told him that John the Baptist was to be born. When Zechariah doubted the news he had brought, the angel found it necessary to punish him; he would lose the power of speech until after the miracle had occurred. Gabriel knows who he is and who he represents when he says *'I am Gabriel. I stand in the presence of God, and I have been sent to speak to you'* (Lk 1, 19).

The well-known words *'Greetings favoured one! The Lord is with you'* (Lk 1, 28), link Gabriel to the greatest mystery in the Redemption story. It was he who was sent to Mary to announce that God would descend to earth through her.

Gabriel's bowed posture shows that this icon probably had its origin in the deesis range on an iconostasis. Michael and Gabriel are portrayed there as intercessors, together with Mary, John the Baptist and other saints.

The Assembly
of the Archangels

Greek version. Egg tempera on beech.
Burnished gold. 45 x 65 cm (1999)

The icon called *The Assembly of the Archangels* (in Greek *synaxis*) is iconographical type probably originating after the iconoclastic period as a symbol of the triumph of Orthodoxy. The feast of the archangels is celebrated on the 8th of November.

The icon shows a solemn group of angels – in this case the three who are mentioned by name in the Scriptures: Michael, Raphael and Gabriel. They are gathered round a medallion of Christ Pantocrator, venerating his image. Our attention is immediately drawn towards the circular icon of Christ which occupies the centre of the composition. Michael and Gabriel, shown with slightly bowed heads and staffs in their hands, hold the medallion between them, while Rafael is depicted frontally, standing behind the medallion. The symmetrical design contributes to the impression of order and deep concentration.

Their clothing is similar to what soldiers and highly ranked servants at the Byzantine court would wear: chiton (tunic), lacerna (short tunic) and chlamyde (cloak). Like all Byzantine angels they have haloes, headbands, curly hair and wings.

In the letter to the Hebrews, angels are described as *'ministering spirits sent forth to serve, for the sake of those who are to obtain salvation'* (Heb 1, 14). The angels are bodiless spirits who live in the immediate presence of God and serve him. They mediate between heaven and earth, being sent to chosen people as messengers, protectors and guides.

Michael is known as commander of the heavenly hosts and as destroyer of the evil powers. Gabriel is associated with divine messages like the annunciation to Mary and Zechariah. Rafael is mentioned in the book of Tobit as a healer, guide and companion. After he had fulfilled his mission, he disclosed his actual identity and presented himself as a celestial being:

'All these days I merely appeared to you and did not eat or drink, but you were seeing a vision' (Tob 12, 19).

Clearly inspired by Neo-Platonic philosophy, Dionysius the Areopagite, an influential monastic writer and mystic from late antiquity, developed a complex angelology where he systematised the angels according to their function and nearness to God. In his famous work *The Celestial Hierarchies,* he ranges them into nine different spheres. Every sphere influences the next in a perpetual stream of energies emanating from the very essence of God himself.

According to the first order, the Seraphim (1) *'occupies a more exalted place than all the others, being immediately present with God'.* Their name means *'those who kindle or make hot'.* The prophet Isaiah, who saw the seraphim in a vision, says that *'each had six wings: with two he covered his face, and with two he covered his feet, and with two he flew'* (Is 6, 2). The Cherubim (2) are characterised as *'knowledge and loving wisdom'.* After the fall, God *'drove out the man; and at the east of the garden of Eden he placed the Cherubim, and a flaming sword which turned every way, to guard the way to the tree of life'* (Gen 3, 24). In a prayer the psalmist urges: *'You who dwell between the Cherubim, shine forth!'* (Ps 80, 1). The Thrones (3) might be identified with the awe-inspiring vehicles referred to by the prophet Ezekiel. They look like wheels equipped with wings and eyes.

In the middle order, we first find the Dominions (4). They are described as *'true Lords'* who exercise *'freedom from all that what is from the earth; they do not turn towards vain shadows'.*

The Virtues (5) personify divine qualities like courage and humility, and bestow these on human beings. The name of the Powers (6) *'signifies the regulation of intellectual and supermundane power which never debases its authority by tyrannical force'.*

Concerning the Principalities (7) in the last order it is said that *'they are wholly turned towards the Prince of Princes, and lead others in princely fashion'.* The Archangels (8), who are seven in number, lead the multitude of angels (9) who are placed below them. Dionysius states that *'their choir is more directly in contact with manifested and mundane things'.* Among these we find the so called guardian angels about whom Christ says that they *'always behold the face of my Father who is in heaven'* (Mt 18, 10).

Sts Peter and Paul

Greek variant.
Egg tempera on oak.
Burnished gold with punching.
24.5 x 29.5 cm
(1993)

Despite the schematic form which also characterises this icon, we get the impression that Peter and Paul have been portrayed with strong individual features. On a Roman medallion from c. 150 AD Peter and Paul are depicted in profile. With such distinctive personal characterisation it seems natural to ask if reproductions could be based on actual observations that were passed on. Peter is portrayed with short, curly hair and a beard, while Paul has a high forehead, a narrow face and a long wavy beard. These attributes became established in orthodox iconography and gradually part of the iconographic canon.

Even though Peter denied his Lord, and Paul had a past as a fanatic persecutor of Christians, they were called upon to be leaders of the apostles. The simple fisherman from Galilee and the learned Pharisee from Tarsus were very dissimilar, both as individuals and as regards social background. Paul tells us of heated confrontations between the two of them, but also of concord and brotherhood. During the debate at the first Church meeting in Jerusalem Peter defended Paul.

On this icon they embrace each other, and in doing so demonstrate how essential unity is, if the Church is to gain credibility. The icon illustrates Peter's own exhortation – to live in accordance with God's will:

'And above all maintain constant love for one another for love covers a multitude of sins'
(1 Pet 4, 8).

THE MYSTICAL LANGUAGE OF ICONS

St Paul

Greek variant.
Egg tempera on oak.
20 x 25 cm (1991)

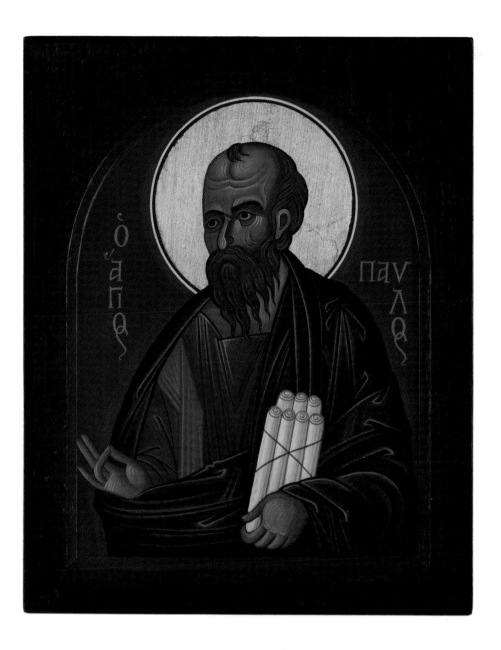

Paul, the zealous apostle and missionary to the heathens, wrote most of the letters in the New Testament – he is responsible for 13 of the 21 letters. On this icon he is portrayed with a bundle of scrolls in his left hand. He holds his right hand as if he were about to give a blessing, but this position may also be interpreted as a gesture made in teaching. Just like the other texts in the New Testament, the letters Paul wrote have been given canonical status; they are to be understood as being divinely inspired. Moreover, Paul lived according to what he preached which is why his words have such great authority.

On the letters Paul writes, Peter comments thus: *'There are some things in them hard to understand, which the ignorant and unstable twist to their own destruction, as they do the other Scriptures'* (2 Pet 3, 16).

Paul ended his life as a martyr in Rome and like John the Baptist was beheaded. Towards the end of his life Paul had reached such an advanced stage in spiritual development and godliness that he was able to say: *'For to me, living is Christ and dying is gain'* (Phil 1, 21). Only a man with the consuming objective of being united with God speaks thus. Such fulfilment may come suddenly, like a mystical experience, or gradually, as the result of a sanctifying process (*theosis*) which begins in this life and continues on into the next. It is this very holiness which is the mark of a saint.

Gregory of Nyssa (c. 335-394) wrote: *'No limit has been set for ascending closer towards God. For there is no limit to goodness, as longing for goodness does not cease with being satisfied.'*

St John the Theologian

Bulgarian variant.
Egg tempera on oak.
24 x 35 cm (1993)

In the Eastern Church, John the Evangelist was often spoken of as *John the Theologian* because his writings showed such deep insight into the divine mysteries. According to tradition John was the youngest of the disciples, and he even refers five times to himself as 'the disciple Jesus loves.' John's head lay on Jesus' breast at the Last Supper, and at the Crucifixion he stood beneath the cross with Mary and later took her home with him. John has rightly been called *The Apostle of Love.*

The ageing, visionary John looks thoughtful – as if he were gazing into the spiritual world. He strokes his chin with his left hand, a gesture which gives him the air of listening and meditating. In his right hand he holds an open book

to his breast and with his index finger points to the opening words of his own gospel, the so-called prologue: *'In the beginning was the Word, and the Word was with God, and the Word was God'* (Jn 1, 1).

Unlike the other apostles, John did not suffer a martyr's death, but was exiled to the island of Patmos. He tells us that: *'I was in the spirit on the Lord's day, and I heard behind me a loud voice like a trumpet'* (Rev 1, 10).

The icon on the right shows how John turns towards the voice. The symbol for Divine Revelation is in the top left corner in the form of spherical circles and beams of light. John listens and passes on what he hears to a writer whom tradition has given the name Prochorus.

THE MYSTICAL LANGUAGE OF ICONS

St John at Patmos

Russian variant. Novgorod school.
Egg tempera on oak. 54 x 59.5 cm (1989)

He sits bent over his work – in front of a dark grotto that symbolises the state of ignorant man. Prochorus, who has an inferior position to John, is sitting in the corner on the right and appears small beside his spiritual master. Nevertheless he resembles his master in being humble and receptive and he also has a halo.

When the most important person is placed in the central position and is unnaturally big compared to the surroundings, the convention denoting different status is being observed. A conspicuous diagonal line has its source in the light beams in the upper left corner, and continues on down through John's face and shoulder to leave his body through his outstretched hand which he lays on Prochorus' head. Here the icon teaches us that God breaks into the created world and reveals himself in an active and discernible way. It also says something about the capacity man has to understand such a message and to grow in spiritual insight.

St Makarios of Egypt

Russian variant. Novgorod school.
Egg tempera on driftwood. 12 x 25.5 cm (1989)

Makarios of Egypt (c. 300-390) also called *the Great*, was one of the first monks to settle in Sketis in the Egyptian wilderness. He represented a simple, down to earth spirituality and emphasised direct experience of God. The radical, ascetic way of life of the Desert Fathers was the ideal and, their spiritual advice was given great authority. This spirituality is known as experiential mysticism – in contrast to the more intellectual trend represented by Evagrios of Pontos (c. 345-399).

Makarios was a contemporary of Anthony the Great (251-356) and was supposed to have met him at least twice. Anthony is considered the founder of the monastic movement and is known for his fearless and persevering struggle against the evil powers – both within and outside himself.

Texts which were earlier attributed to Makarios of Egypt, are now linked to a Syrian monk (Pseudo-Makarios) proficient in Greek. However, the content of these texts reflects a spirituality which conforms with the spirit of the 'genuine' Makarios.

Homily 5, 8:

The immaterial and divine fire illuminates the soul and puts it to the test. This fire descended on the apostles in the form of tongues of flame. This fire shone before Paul, it spoke to him, it illuminated his mind and at the same time blinded his eyes, for the flesh cannot endure the brightness of this light. Moses saw this fire in the burning bush. This fire lifted Elijah from the ground in the form of a flaming chariot.

Homily 34, 1:

But above all the eyes of the soul must be fixed on Christ, who, like a good painter, paints in those who believe in him and constantly behold him, a portrait of the heavenly man, in his own image, by means of the Holy Spirit, out of the very substance of his ineffable light.

Homily 5, 8:

In so far as each has been counted worthy through faith and diligence to become a partaker of the Holy Spirit, to the same extent his body also shall be glorified in that day. For what the soul has now stored up within, shall then be revealed and displayed outwardly in the body.

Homily 5, 9:

At the day of resurrection the glory of the Holy Spirit comes out from within, adorning and covering the bodies of the saints with the glory which they had before, but hidden within their souls. What a man has now, the same then comes out of the the body. Their bodies shall be glorified through the unspeakable light which even now is within them – that is, the power of the Holy Spirit.

St Nicholas of Myra

Greek variant
Egg tempera on beech. 17 x 28 cm (1993)

Bishop Nicholas of Myra, also called *The Miracle worker,* was born to a well-off family in the town of Patara in Asia Minor between 240 and 245. He died on 6th December, probably in 326.

During the persecution of Christians by Diocletian early in the 300s, Nicholas was put in chains and exiled. He was among around 300 bishops who took part in a General Council in Nicaea in 325 where the Nicene Creed was formulated. This Creed settled a conflict regarding Arianism – a heretical teaching which did not recognise the divine nature of Christ. The priest Arius (ca 260-336) maintained that Christ was a higher created being, a kind of superman with unique moral and spiritual qualities. As a reaction against this, the council fathers defined the relationship between the divine and human natures of Christ in a concise and at the same time poetic manner:

> *God from God, Light from Light*
> *true God, from true God.*
> *Begotten not made,*
> *of one being with the Father*
> *Through him all things were made*
> *For us men and for our Salvation*
> *he came down from heaven:*
> *by the power of the Holy Spirit he*
> *became incarnate from the Virgin Mary*
> *and became man.*

When we see Nicholas in some icons portrayed with a sword in his hand, it is a symbol of the conflict against Arianism.

Nicholas is best known for his many miracles and good deeds. Among other things it is said that one night he helped a poor man who could not afford dowries for his three daughters by throwing three nuggets of gold through his open window. The custom of giving children presents in a stocking on the evening of 5th December comes from this episode.

Nicholas carried out his charitable deeds discreetly. He showed fellow feeling and gave alms without embarrassing the recipients.

Once Nicholas intervened and stopped three innocent men from being executed. After a meeting with the bishop, the person responsible became a convert – and begged forgiveness.

On a pilgrimage to the Holy Land, the boat he was on ran into a heavy storm, but Nicholas prayed to God and the threatening sea became calm. After this Christ-like miracle, Nicholas became the patron saint for seafarers. Innumerable churches and chapels dedicated to this saint have been raised by thankful fishermen and seamen who have returned safely home from the sea.

Because of the Islamic conquest of the Byzantine empire, the relics of St Nicholas were rescued – or stolen – by Italian seamen in 1087 and transferred from Myra to Bari in South Italy. There a new grave church was built in honour of the saint. The feast day of St Nicholas is celebrated 6th December both in the Eastern and the Western traditions.

The legendary American Santa Clause originated from Protestant traditions surrounding Sinte Klaus (Nicholas) and was introduced to the country by Dutch immigrants. This commercial variant of a kind old man eventually returned to Europe.

St Simeon the Stylite

Russian variant. Novgorod School.
Egg tempera on oak. 24.3 x 40 cm)

Simeon the Stylite (300-459) practised an extreme form of asceticism in keeping with the ideals of the Desert Fathers. But Simeon went even further than his predecessors in his search to live a life centred on God. He did not seek somewhere in the wilderness to live, but installed himself on a pillar on the outskirts of Antioch. To keep an even greater distance from the people who crowded around to see him, he kept on building his pillar higher and higher, until it was 18 metres above the ground.

Great crowds of people made pilgrimages to the holy man to ask him for spiritual guidance and also to ask him to act as intercessor to God on their behalf. The inner peace that radiated from him acted as magnet. He demonstrated the truth in the words which the Russian elder (starets) Serafim of Sarov (1759-1833) spoke ca 1400 years later: *'Have peace in your heart, and thousands will come to you.'*

When Simeon the Stylite died in 459, he had lived continually for more than 30 years on top of the pillar. With his almost supernatural way of life, he pointed towards the boundlessness of the world to come.

In this icon Simeon is depicted in the traditional robes which characterises the Orthodox hermit. His right hand is raised in blessing and in his left hand he holds a scroll. Apart from the robes, these attributes are reminiscent of how Christ is portrayed in Orthodox iconography. Like all other saints the stylite is also an imitator of Christ, one who gradually lets himself be transformed into a greater likeness of his model. The curious features of this form of spirituality might easily conceal the timeless aspect which is also implicit in this saint's life story.

The hexagonal opening at the top of the pillar is filled by the upper part of Simeon's body, but the composition does not allow for any natural placement for the rest of it. In all Ortodox iconography the architecture or the landscape functions as a setting for the event, which is why the figure is not in proper proportion to the surroundings.

The box-like construction Simeon lived in is in inverse perspective, as is the stairway leading up to the pillar. Both of these elements are seen from above, while Simeon himself is portrayed frontally. The inconsistent use of perspective is yet another illogical feature that heightens the meaning of the symbolic content.

An icon is always more than an illustration. The event or person represented in an icon has a relevance far beyond the concrete situation. An icon shall not only reproduce an historic reality; in this instance it concerns an ascetic in Syria who spent many years on a pillar sometime during the fourth century. It shall also show the transcendental reality the saint reflects in his earthly life which people of our time may also understand. These spiritual qualities are realised to a great degree through liturgical celebrations of the saint's memorial day. In the Orthodox calendar, Simeon is celebrated on 1st September.

THE MYSTICAL LANGUAGE OF ICONS

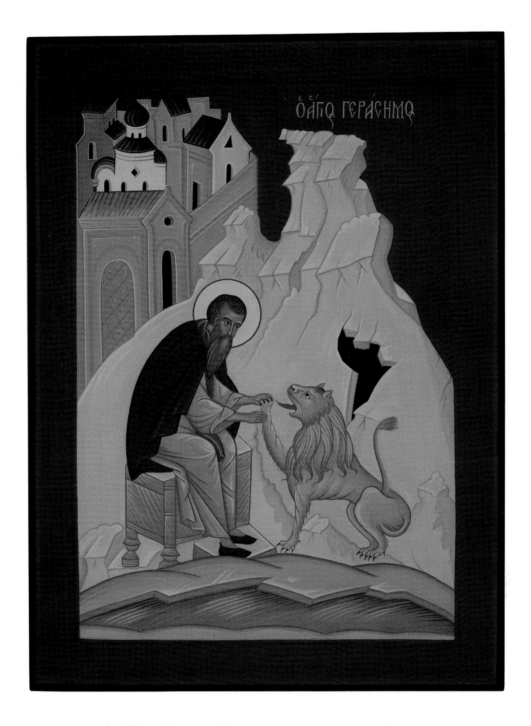

St Gerasimos and the Lion

Russian variant. Egg tempera on oak. 31 x 42 cm (1998)

It has been told that Gerasimos was the abbot of a monastery in Jordan. He died in 475. One day a lion with a splinter in one of its front paws limped up to Gerasimos and sat down in front of him. The icon depicts the lion lifting up its paw to Gerasimos so he can take out the splinter. To show its thanks, the lion is supposed to have served Gerasimos for the rest of its life.

The literature about the saints gives many examples of wild animals living in peaceful harmony with holy ascetics. It is as if animals sense that the saints represent the laws found in another and better life. Such episodes may be interpreted as an image of the harmony that reigned between Adam and the animals in the Garden of Eden – or as a glimpse of the perfect life in the coming world. St Paul has this eschatological perspective in mind when he writes that *'the creation waits with eager longing for the revealing of the children of God'* (Rom 8, 19).

St Mary of Egypt

Italian-Byzantine variant. Egg tempera on mahogany.
Burnished gold. 16 x 33 cm (1993)

Mary of Egypt (354-421), who was later given the name *The Penitent*, lived as a prostitute in the port of Alexandria for 17 years, from when she was 12 until she was 29. In 383 she joined a group of pilgrims on their way to Jerusalem by ship. During the journey and in Jerusalem she carried on her trade.

On the day of the Elevation of the Holy Cross, Mary wanted to go into the church grave with the pilgrims to see the relics displayed there. However, when she reached the threshold, she was held back by an invisible force. At the same time she caught sight of an icon of Mary, the

Mother of God, and was filled with remorse over the sinful life she had led. After she had converted and asked The Mother of God for help, nothing stopped her entering the church and kneeling before the cross.

Sometime later she took three loaves of bread and a crock of water and moved out into the desert, east of the river Jordan. There she began to live as a hermit under extremely ascetic conditions. After having lived alone for 47 years in the most inaccessible part of the desert, she was discovered by the priest Zosima. He believed it might be a spirit or an angel he saw. He was amazed at finding a living being so far out in the wilderness, and was even more amazed when he understood that it was a woman he had found. She was wearing no clothes, but had covered her body with her own hair. At first Mary would not talk to him and hid in a grotto. When Zosima would not give up, but followed her, she at last told him who she was and asked him to bring her communion on the coming Maundy Thursday. He did as she asked and promised to return on the same day the following year. But when he arrived he found her dead, lying with her face towards the east. Beside her head Zosima found some writing in the sand: *'Bury the body of the sinner Mary here.'* The earth was dry and hard, and Zosima who was an old man had not the strength to dig. Suddenly he saw a lion sitting beside Mary's body licking her feet. With its front paws the lion dug out a hole that was deep enough for Zosima to lay Mary to rest.

The dramatic extremes of Mary's life make her a model for conversion and remorse. As well as these basic themes, her life is filled with underlying symbolism. When it is told that she walked on the waters of the Jordan, it may be read as an image of Baptism. She was also supposed to have lived on the bread and water she took with her from Jerusalem for many years. This supernatural phenomenon links Mary to the prophet Elijah and the miracle of oil that was never used up, and also to Jesus' miracle of the bread.

The friendly lion may be a sign that the life the deeply remorseful Mary lived may in some respects be compared to a paradisaical state. But the lion may also symbolise Christ himself, *'the Lion of the tribe of Judah, the Root of David'* (Rev 5, 5).

THE MYSTICAL LANGUAGE OF ICONS

St Gregory Palamas

Russian variant. Egg tempera on mahogany.
Burnished gold. 16 x 33 cm (1993)

Gregory Palamas, archbishop of Thessaloniki (1296-1359) grew up at the Emperor's court in Constantinople where he was given a higher education. As a young man Gregory became the pupil of a spiritual teacher on Athos, a monk who taught Gregory a psycho-physical method of prayer called Hesychasm. The word *hesychia* means tranquillity, concentration and composure.

The Hesychasts interpreted St Paul's encouragement to *'pray without ceasing'* (1 Thess 5, 17) quite literally. By linking a short prayer formula to inhaling and exhaling it was possible to keep attention always centred on God. Those praying focused on the heart (cardia), the centre of personality, and recited *'Jesus Christ, Son of God, have mercy on me a sinner.'* The classical formula, which was later known as the Jesus prayer, comes from a prayer shouted by the blind beggar: *'Jesus, Son of David, have mercy on me!'* – *Kyrie eleison!* – (Lk 18, 38), and the repentant tax-collector: *'God, be merciful to me, a sinner!'* (Lk 18, 13).

Gregory was against certain contemporary sectarian factions whose aim was a dualistic understanding of the world. By despising matter, they also underrated the Incarnation and the sacramental life. Even if the Heyschasts represented a fully tried, contemplative tradition with roots going right back to the Desert Fathers, there was heated dissension about that spirituality in the 1300s. During the conflict over the icons and in the debate about Hesychastic beliefs, the relationship between spirit and matter was a main theme. Gregory builds on the Jewish-Christian creator belief when he argues that matter has an innate sacred capacity – the created is the positive will of God and *'exceedingly good'*, and with the Incarnation, God himself descended into matter and became a man of flesh and blood. Sacraments are material, perceptible signs which perpetuate the fruits of that divine descent.

The Hesychasts maintain that not only the soul, but also the body may become a partaker in divine nature (2 Pet 1, 4). Gregory is known for having reflected deeply over different sides of the Transfiguration of Christ. He was especially engaged with what the uncreated light that became visible on Mount Tabor says about God, man and creation in general. Gregory refers to a liturgical text where it says *'You have revealed an indistinct beam of your divinity'*. He further reminds us that Moses and Stephen experienced a visible transfiguration of the body in their lifetime. This points forward to the corporeal resurrection from the dead: *'The glory of the spirit which shines on the face of the blessed Moses, which no human could bear to look at, indicates through this sign how the bodies of the holy will be glorified after the righteous arise from the dead...'*

'What then of Stephen, the first martyr? While he lived, his face shone like the face of an angel. Did not his body also experience divine things?'

Our Lady of the Sign

Russian variant. Egg tempera on pine. Diameter 47.5 cm (1989)

We feel ourselves compelled to portray
what is characteristic of our faith,
and that is that Christ did not just appear to be a man,
like some kind of shadow,
but that he really and truly was a man.

Germanus of Constantinople.

Mandylion

Polish variant. Egg tempera on oak. Burnished gold. 47.5 x 22 cm (1988)

REVIEWS

'For Solrunn Nes icon painting is an expression of her faith, and the religious dimension is therefore essential. Nevertheless it is important that it is the icon that links beauty with truth and goodness to an indissoluble whole. The icon's beauty can elicit a longing in the viewer, and at the same time present this longing to its object: God, ie, the Truth. This truth is the dogma of the Church that is mediated through a tradition which Solrunn Nes feels part of. That truth is something else and more than a subjective feeling is important to her. In short, the tradition in which she paints is not concerned with what the painter subjectively understands as truth. What is important is that church dogma is expressed in fixed norms for design, with the good clearly defined: that which is of God and leads to fellowship with him.

The icon painter shall not write a personal gospel, but like a pianist give the composition a loyal, artistic rendering. The pianist must have musicality in the widest sense of the word, the same applies to the icon painter. The work exhibited fully documents that Solrunn Nes has such musicality.'

Henrik von Aachen. Senior Curator,
in the catalogue 'Images of another Reality'
Icon Exhibition at Bergen Museum, 10.11.89 - 07.01.90

'The icon's stylised beauty, holy figures in dignified seriousness against a burnished gold background, can invite any one to contemplation, even if one is not familiar with the strict requirements of content and form to which icons are subject.'

Sissel Hamre Dagsland, Bergens Tidende. 14.11.89.

'First and foremost, the paintings of Solrunn Nes are typical of the epic style, a legendary narrative presentation which builds upon Biblical ground, but is still given a personal interpretation. There are a number of representations of the Mother of God who bore the child Jesus as a divine being. In her work the artist reconciles the Antique and the Oriental as is seen in her independent compositions.

Sensitivity to line in portraying bodies and clothing is outstanding, as is the feel for harmonic grouping, which suggests a classical influence. Just as in the other icon paintings the dominant motif is Christ Pantocrator, Ruler of All, painted in the Greek style. Icon theology in Byzantium from the 700s to the late Middle Ages is adapted, but with modern methods and contemporary interpretation.

This icon exhibition is without question a pearl in the large jubilee exhibition "In Honour of God and the Virgin Mary", an ideal not least, that the interpretations of the iconography by Solrunn Nes live up to.'

Ewe Olsson, Östgöta Correspondenten, 31.05.96.
Bjälbopalatset i Vadstena

SOLRUNN NES

AUTHOR BIOGRAPHY

Education:
Basic Psychology course 1982
Trained in Russian icon painting, Finland 1983
Basic course in History of Religions 1984
Greek State Scolarship 1985
Academy of Fine Arts, Athens
Main subject in Art History 1992
Basic Greek course 1994

Exhibitions:
Bryggen Museum, Bergen 1985
Kampen Church, Stavanger 1986
Galleri 1814, Eidsvoll 1987
Bergen Museum, Bergen 1989
Molde Kunstforening 1990
Drengestova at Nes 1990
Tao Fong Shan, Hong Kong 1990
Volda Kunstforening 1991
Nordenfjeldske Kunstindustimuseum,
Trondheim 1991
Ringerike Museum 1992
Haugesund KFUM 1992
Aylesford Priory, Kent 1993
Westminster Cathedral, London 1993
St. Magnus Church, Lillestrøm 1993
Galleri Rosendal 1994
Vereide Church 1995
Gort Muire, Dublin 1995
Bjälbopalatset, Vadstena 1996
Kvam Kunstlag 1996
Galleri Siverts, Bergen 1997
Galleri Krogh, Vestnes 1997

Decorations:
Transfiguration icon, Aylesford Priory,
England 1989
Crucifix, Takvam Chapel, Arna 1990
Prosessional Cross, Church for the Deaf,
Bergen 1990
Crucifix and altar frontal,
St Paul Catholic Church, Bergen 1991
Reconstruction of Gothic altar frontal,
Hamre Church, Osterøy 1995
Colouring and guilding of crucifix,
Fantoft New Stavechurch 1997
Reconstruction of Gothic altar frontal,
Tjugum Church, Balestrand 1997

BIBLIOGRAPHY

Baggley, John, *Doors of Perception – icons and their spiritual significance,* Mowbray, Oxford & London 1987

Cennino d'Andrea Cennini, *The Craftman's Handbook,* Translated by Daniel V. Thompson, Jr. Dover Publications, Inc., New York

Damascus, St John of, *On the Divine Images,* Saint Vladimir's Seminary Press, New York 1987

de Caluwé, Robert, *Ikonenmalerei,* Rosenheimer Raritäten, Rosenheim 1984

Dionysius the Areopagite, *The Mystical Theology and the Celestial Hierarchies,* The Shrine of Wisdom, Surrey 1965

Evdokimov, Paul, *The Art of the Icon: a theology of beauty,* Oakwood Publications, California 1990 (1972)

Frye, Northrop, *The Great Code, The Bible and Literature,* Harcourt Brace Jovanovich Publishers, New York & London 1982 (1981)

Gregory Palamas, *The Triads,* The Classics of Western Spirituality, Paulist Press, New York 1983

Hetherington, Paul, *'The Painter's Manual' of Dionysius of Fourna,* The Sagittarius Press, London 1974

Haustein-Bartsch, Eva, *Ikonen-Museum Recklinghausen,* Deutscher Kunstverlag, München 1995

Lossky, Vladimir, *The Mystical Theology of the Eastern Church,* James Clarke, Cambridge & London 1973 (1957)

Lowden, John, *Early Christian & Byzantine Art,* Phaidon Press Limited, London 1997

Mango, Cyril, *The Art of the Byzantine Empire, 312-1453, Sources and Documents,* in the series *Sources and Documents in the History of Art,* edited by H.W. Janson, Prentice Hall, Englewood Cliffs, New Jersey 1972

Onasch, Konrad, *Die Ikonenmalerei,* Koehler & Amelang, Leipzig 1967

Onasch, Konrad, *Kunst und Liturgie der Ostkirche,* Koehler & Amelang, Leipzig 1967

Onasch, Konrad & Schnieper, Annemarie, *Ikonen, Faszination und Wirklichkeit,* EBM-Service für Verleger, Luzern, Schweiz 1995

Ouspensky, Leonid, Theology of the Icon, Saint Vladimir's Seminary Press, New York 1978

Ouspensky, Leonid & Lossky, Vladimir, *The Meaning of Icons,* Saint Vladimir's Seminary Press, New York 1982 (1952)

Pseudo-Macarius, The Fifty Spiritual Homilies and the Great Letter, The Classics of Western Spirituality, Paulist Press, New York 1992

Quenot, Michel, *The Resurrection and the Icon,* Saint Vladimir's Seminary Press, New York 1997

Ramos-Poquí, Guillem, *The Technique of Icon Painting,* Burns & Oates / Search Press, Kent 1990

Sahas, Daniel J., *Icon and Logos, Sources in Eighth Century Iconoclasm,* University of Toronto Press, Toronto, Buffalo, London 1988 (1986)

Sendler, Egon, S.J. *The Icon, Image of the Invisible, Elements of Theology, Aesthetics and Technique*, Oakwood Publications, California 1993 (1988)

Studite, St Theodore the, *On the Holy Icons*, Saint Vladimir's Seminary Press, New York 1981

Talbot Rice, David, *Art of the Byzantine Era*, Thames & Hudson, London 1977 (1963)

The Holy Bible, Revised Standard Version, Catholic Edition, Ignatius Press, San Francisco

The Lenten Triodion and the Festal Menaion, translated by Mother Mary and Kallistos Ware, St Tikhon's Seminary Press, Pennsylvania 1998

The Lost Books of the Bible and The Forgotten Books of Eden, A Meridian Book, New American Library, Times Mirror, New York and Scarborough, Ontario 1974 (1927)

Ward, Benedicta, S.L.G., *Harlots of the Desert: A study of repentance in early monastic sources*, Mowbray, London & Oxford 1987

Ware, Kallistos, *The Ortodox Way*, Mowbray, Oxford & London 1979

Yannaras, Christos, *Elements of Faith: An introduction to Orthodox Theology*, T&T Clark, Worcester 1991